The Gift

Had My Life Just Begun?

PHIL COLEMAN

BALBOA.
PRESS
A DIVISION OF HAY HOUSE

Balboa Press books may be ordered through booksellers or by contacting:

Balboa Press
A Division of Hay House
1663 Liberty Drive
Bloomington, IN 47403
www.balboapress.com
1 (877) 407-4847

Print information available on the last page.

ISBN: 978-1-5043-7809-3 (sc)
ISBN: 978-1-5043-7811-6 (hc)
ISBN: 978-1-5043-7810-9 (e)

Library of Congress Control Number: 2017905479

Balboa Press rev. date: 04/25/2017

This book is dedicated to my amazing sister, Lin, who gave me my life back with the wonderful gift that changed me forever. This book is also dedicated to my mother, Magdalene Coleman. I would never have been able to cope with the early years on dialysis without your support and courage. You will not be forgotten.

Acknowledgements

I would like to acknowledge the support that I have received from all my family and friends during my life. I thank them for being there for me along the journey.

In particular, I would like to thank the doctors and nurses who have supported me and helped me survive the challenges.

Contents

Introduction

You might ask: Why have I written this book?

Well, I hope that someone, one day, will read it and realise that even though living with kidney failure brings a lot of challenges, you can still have a great life.

The ability to live with any type of chronic illness comes down to support from your family and friends, and a bit of stubbornness on your own part. The reason I say stubbornness is because it is up to you, at the end of the day, to decide to make the best of your life. No one can force you to enjoy yourself. I have found that developing a positive attitude by focusing on the good times is very important.

After being diagnosed with kidney failure, I discovered life can be as varied and exciting as I want. Given the circumstances that are laid out before you with any chronic illness, you may think that it is a hell of a challenge and that you can't do it. My hope is that this book will give you insight into my life: what I have been through, what I have and haven't achieved, and how I have felt while experiencing what I have. Understand that no matter what happens, you can still have a great life with a chronic condition. The hardest things to do are keeping focused on what you want and staying positive!

One of the first things you are likely to find out after being diagnosed with chronic illness is that there are several treatment options you and your consultant may consider, especially if you are diagnosed early enough. One of the first major challenges that you will be faced with will be making these treatment decisions.

In the case of kidney disease, these treatments were among my choices:

- Medication and dietary control – following a renal diet and taking medication to support the body, to delay the need for dialysis or transplantation.
- Haemodialysis – a process that uses a man-made membrane (dialyzer/artificial kidney) to remove wastes, such as urea, from the blood. This process restores the proper balance of electrolytes in the blood and eliminates extra fluid from the body.
- Peritoneal dialysis – a process that uses the lining of the abdominal cavity (peritoneal membrane) and a solution (dialysate) to remove wastes and extra fluid from the body.
- Kidney transplantation – a surgical procedure to place a kidney from a live or deceased donor into a person whose kidneys no longer function properly.

These treatments were the only ones I was aware of for kidney failure at the time of writing this book. A combination of treatments was also an option.

Whatever your condition, and whatever your treatment options, *a consultant is best suited to recommend the treatment that is right for you.*

Prologue

Life Before

Before I go further, there is one thing I'd like to say about this book: I don't want people to read into the text anything apart from what is there. I am a pretty simple bloke. What you read is what I meant, straight down the line, with nothing hidden.

Support from family and friends helped me to stay positive and focused. My dad, John Iream Coleman, was a great role model for me as he was throughout his life, including service in a world war.

When I was born, Dad was 50 years old, but he could always pass for a man ten years younger – which he did on many occasions to gain employment. He had a full head of silver-grey hair, dyed black occasionally. He was nearly six feet tall and always dressed well. He even wore a tie at home, unless he was working in his greenhouse, whether on his latest invention or a new hybrid plant.

Dad was a very intelligent man and always had a fresh idea on the drawing board. I remember when we lived in Canberra, Dad started looking into how different spectra of light affected plant growth. From that idea he moved into experimenting with fibre optics. I never found out what that experiment was about, but I would not be surprised if it was about transmitting signals through the fibres. I am sure he got some of his ideas from where he was working at that stage, the Auroral Valley Tracking Station. Dad would have loved growing up with the technology of the twenty-first century!

His life had been difficult, and yet he survived and managed to make sure that his wife and children were secure. He was very British and old-fashioned. One of his favourite sayings was 'Stiff upper lip, son; things could be worse', especially if he didn't know what else to say.

He also used to say, 'See how you feel after a shower, son,' when I wasn't feeling well in mornings, during the months before I went on dialysis. Dad was very caring but also very strict in his approach to raising his children. In this day and age, some may consider him too strict. But, thinking back, both Mum and Dad always had my best interests at heart. They may not have really understood what I was going through, but they tried their best. Without support from them, my brothers, and my sister, I would not be writing this book today.

I was born in Durban, South Africa, to a middle-class couple. My father was a sales manager. My mother, Magdalene Elinor, was initially a housewife; then she started working in Australia. Mum married Dad when she was 20 and Dad was 40 years old.

I was the youngest of five full siblings. Pearse was the eldest, Josh second, Luke the middle child, and Lin (Elinor) the second youngest. I was to find out when I was 19 that my father had another son, Roderick, from a previous marriage, so there were six of us in total.

When we were kids in South Africa, Mum always looked after us. She bandaged the wounds from all our accidents and was supportive. Dad was very much the strict authority figure when he had to be, but he was also the crazy inventor we had so much fun with.

As the years went by my parents' roles changed. Mum and Dad both had to work, and there were more shared responsibilities. My relationship with my parents also changed, especially in my later years on dialysis.

Part of my childhood in South Africa is somewhat of a mystery, as I was only six when we left for a new life in Australia. We were pretty cute kids during our years in South Africa, even if I do say myself.

The Coleman Clan

At the time we left South Africa, I had only just started my first term of primary school at King Edward School in Johannesburg, which my brothers also attended. The most I can recall of that school is that the classroom was dark and dingy, but the teacher was very friendly. When I left, the class gave me a farewell party, and my teacher gave me a bookmark. I still have it somewhere. I never really used it, as I didn't develop a passion for reading like my father and mother. They were avid readers.

We lived in Johannesburg for most of my childhood in South Africa. When we started our trip to Australia, in May 1967, we caught a train from Johannesburg to Durban. Mum and the five kids, carrying three cold chickens for food, did the overnight trip. We all brought bedrolls – one of Dad's great ideas which worked out very well in the end. This was my first big trip, let alone the fact that I had never been on a train or a ship. As a 6-year-old, I was pretty excited.

When we arrived in Durban, we boarded a ship, the *Northern Star*, pretty well straight away. I loved the ship and soon knew all its shortcuts. It was my playground for about a month. I could smell the diesel from the engine room sometimes as I moved around the ship, especially the lower decks.

I played a game with my family by letting them take the normal route to the dining room while I dashed off on a short cut to beat them. The only times it was a bit dangerous were when I tried to go outside during storms. The gangways got very slippery.

Our accommodation was pretty cramped, but we managed. We used our bedrolls on the bunks, which made it feel more like home. The bunks reminded me of the ones in the old movies. They were metal and built into the side of the ship. There wasn't a lot of floor space, and the bathroom was down the corridor. I don't think any of us spent much time in the cabins; they were just places to sleep at the end of the day. Mum, Dad, Lin, and I had one cabin, and Pearse, Josh, and Luke shared another. Each cabin had one small porthole, which was above the waterline, thankfully.

The quality of the food on the ship was good, and we never were hungry. There was only one time I can remember when dinner was cancelled, and that was because of a storm tossing the ship around. The tables and chairs had to be tied down.

When we arrived in Perth, there was nobody there to meet us. We were immigrants, and no one seemed to be interested. Pearse wasn't impressed about having to carry his bedroll down the gangplank, but Dad made each of us carry our own. As it took us a while to disembark and there were a lot of people waiting and watching on the Fremantle Wharf, I think Pearse was a bit embarrassed. We all felt a bit like ducks out of water, arriving in a new country. I expected to see a kangaroo hopping up to meet us. After all, I was only 6 years old, and it *was* Australia.

Mum and Dad had arranged for us to stay in a migrants' hostel for a few nights. We looked for more permanent accommodation, and we also needed to buy a car. Dad organised the car within a few days of our arrival. We went for our first drive around the city, all seven of us in a Morris Minor. Dad always tried to make our trips a bit of fun, and this trip included our first taste of Australian fish and chips – with Coke, of course. It was delicious!

Dad found us a house soon after getting the car. The suburb that we moved to was called Wembley. I started primary school there with Luke and Lin. I fit in pretty well with the other kids, although there were always some who wanted to make an issue about us coming from South Africa.

One day I made a stupid mistake. I was trying to act smart and walk home by myself. When I crossed the main road, I was apparently hit by a car. I only remember passing out in the middle of the road. I woke up under the radiator of a car. The driver took Luke, Lin, and me home. I was fine, or at least had no broken bones. I think I was a bit of a brat when I was a kid. Luckily, Dad never found out, as he would have punished me severely for not staying with Luke.

Dad got a sales job pretty quickly. Things were going well, and we moved soon after to another suburb called Woodlands. While I was at Woodlands Primary, I had my first real crush on a girl in my class. I can't believe that I still remember her name. I won't give it, as I have no idea where she is and I don't think she realised it anyway. She was gorgeous. Of course, I was just a 'friend' to her.

We stayed at Woodlands until I was in fifth grade. I had my first taste of music there. I saw mankind walk on the moon. I also got into heaps of trouble. One year my class went through five teachers. I don't think they could claim we went through all those teachers because of our antics, but we certainly had fun in our group. I must admit I was never what you might call a conscientious student.

During my fifth grade year, Dad was offered a job to manage the Auroral Valley Tracking Station near Canberra, and he took it. He wanted a change, and the salary was better. Whenever we had a major change in our family, Dad called for a 'round table', which meant that we all sat around the dining room table to hear what Mum and Dad had decided. I don't think anything we kids could have said would have changed our parents' minds; however, it was our introduction to a form of democracy.

A few years before we moved to Canberra, my eldest brother Pearse decided to join the navy. It was always good to see him when he was on shore leave, but I can't remember if he was involved in the discussions to move. I am sure his input wouldn't have changed anything either.

I wasn't happy about leaving my friends behind. On the other hand, I was also excited about seeing a new city and meeting new people. I have always had a bit of a traveller's attitude, and you never really get hurt when you need to move on.

Our trip to Canberra was by plane. Unfortunately, there was an airline strike on the weekend that we needed to fly, so we had to stop over in Melbourne for several hours. We were exhausted, so Dad arranged for us to crash at a hotel near the airport. We all piled into the only room available; it was pretty crazy.

In the morning, Dad organised breakfast. It was massive. I have never seen so much food eaten so ravenously by our family. It was like a pack of hyenas devouring a kill. We also went to a bar. Mom and the kids had Coke on the rocks, while Dad and Pearse each had a beer. We watched a band rehearse. It was a great trip.

In Canberra, I went to a fantastic primary school, Red Hill Primary. Lin, Luke, and Josh went to Narrabundah High. I ended up dropping back a year to fourth grade. In those days, the curriculum weren't the same across the states, and I had never studied a lot of what was being taught in their fifth grade classrooms.

Of course I got a crush, but this time on one of the teachers – Mrs V, who was my swimming teacher. The crush was very distracting and probably was the reason why I never really learned to swim. But she was always around to save me from drowning. She was very attractive: tall, with long, dark hair and a figure like the lead actress from *Xena: Warrior Princess*. Check out the series and you will see what I mean. Yes, I did like that type of show, including *Hercules*, *Star Wars*, and of course *Star Trek*!

After Red Hill Primary, I went to Telopea Park High for a short time and became friends with an interesting group of kids. Telopea Park High was pretty rough in those days, but the guys I hung around with were cool. We used to get into a bit of trouble, but not as bad as some.

I was only at Telopea Park High for one term before we moved to the other side of Canberra. We had been allocated a government house. I ended up going to Woden Valley High with my sister Lin. This was where I really started playing guitar. I joined my first band with some friends, Ian and Harold. Ian and I played electric guitar, and Harold played bass guitar.

Apart from music, Ian, Harold, and I enjoyed discussing politics and researching World War II. We were primarily interested in facts and stories about the campaigns. From my perspective, it helped me understand my father a bit better. Dad had been deployed to Myanmar (Burma) during the war, so that campaign was of particular interest.

Most weekends we got together and had a jam session. We got pretty good. Ian's mother organised our first gig at her primary school, playing for the fifth graders. We had a great time. All the girls wanted Ian's autograph, but he was the only one to receive that adoration.

I am still good friends with Ian and Harold today. Ian's influence was the main reason I started playing the blues. Several years after our high school exploits, he asked me to join a blues band that he was in, called Blind Freddy, as they needed a singer.

I was introduced to other musicians via my brothers. Pearse and Luke were on their way to their own careers in music. I was just tagging along at that point. They took me to their jam sessions, so I soon perfected playing basic guitar.

My life took a bit of a detour when I was about 13. I had my first introduction to the medical profession. One afternoon I played golf with Harold. When we had finished, we waited for his mum to pick us up. We passed the time by pretending we were in World War II bombers, bombing military targets on the ground. I used a rock as my bomb and some broken bottles as targets. Unfortunately, a sliver of glass flew up into my left eye. I ended up in hospital, but luckily I didn't need an operation. I had to wear patches on my eyes for several weeks, and never got my full sight back in the injured left eye. This detour was minor compared to what was ahead.

After a while, Dad left the Auroral Tracking Station job and went back to sales. Then he got a job managing the Croatian Club in Canberra. Our next move was to Brisbane, where Dad got a better job managing the United Services Club. By this time I was the only child left at home. The job in Brisbane was more pay, and Dad was getting tired of the cold in Canberra, so we moved.

In my view, Brisbane was a bit of a waste of time. I did my school certificate there, which was year 10, and then we moved again, this time to Sydney. Dad had got another job offer at another club. We moved to Sydney at the end of 1977, and I attended Cumberland High School in 1978.

My story really begins in early 1978. We went on a school excursion to the Snowy Mountains. It was great, and I had a good time. When I got back, my left ankle was swollen, so Dad took me to his doctor or general practitioner (GP). This was the first time I had seen a GP, apart from when I got measles as a young child. The GP told Dad that he thought I had a sprained ankle, and he never checked anything else.

I wonder if that GP could have identified that I had kidney failure right then? Could diagnosing kidney failure at that early stage have changed what happened later? What if I had gone on dialysis six months earlier than I did? We will never know.

I don't know how often teenagers see doctors these days, but I think it would be worthwhile for them to have a simple blood test to get a baseline of their general health. This may help identify issues early, especially in cases where there is a history of medical problems in the family. Obviously, this is a personal choice, but I personally don't see the harm in finding out how healthy you are.

1

Had My Life Ended?

For most teenagers in Australia during the 1970s, life was great. They were discovering what life was all about by going to discos, parties, sporting events, and of course the beach.

In 1978, I was 17 years of age. After Dad took me to the GP, my health got progressively worse. I threw up at least once or twice on most days and couldn't hold down any food. I got cramps in my legs and didn't have any energy.

My uncle had a heart attack and passed away in South Africa, so my mum had to go to the funeral and support her family. My brother Pearse moved home to be with my dad. Dad wasn't sure what was wrong with me, just that I was pretty sick.

I got worse, and my dad got more worried. He had a tendency to think that things would be fine and being sick was only temporary. After all, the GP had said that I was fine. Dad tried giving me different food. I believe he thought I might be allergic to what I was eating, possibly because the GP suggested as much.

I saw the GP in May or June. By November, both my ankles were swollen about three times their normal size. I hadn't seen any other doctor at that point, but I was definitely very sick. I had no idea what was going on. It was getting near my exams and I needed to study, but I couldn't focus at all.

The day before my life was turned upside down, I went to school as usual. The first lesson was maths. As I sat down, my teacher said – I thought jokingly – 'You look a bit green today, Phil. Are you OK?' I laughed it off and prepared for the class.

Before the end of the class, a head office representative came into the office and said that Dad had made an appointment for me to see another doctor. I had to meet him at the front office after class.

I was totally unaware of what that appointment would mean for my future. It certainly changed my life.

As my dad drove me to the doctor, he was unaccustomedly quiet. When we got to the surgery, we were taken straight in. The nurse took my blood pressure and I gave a urine sample. After checking out my ankles, the doctor rang the Royal Prince Alfred Hospital to discover when I could see a specialist. He then took a blood sample and told me I needed to stay home from school and come back the next day for the results.

I didn't sleep very well that night; I was throwing up, having leg cramps, and the usual symptoms. At least we were due to see the doctor in the morning. When my dad and I walked into the surgery the next day, the doctor had already arranged me to be admitted to Royal Prince Alfred Hospital Renal Unit for tests. He wanted my dad, who was getting very worried by that stage, to take me to the hospital. We did so after stopping at home so I could pick up the stuff that I thought I would need for one night. I was wrong …

When I was admitted, the medical staff did a whole lot of tests, as they suspected that I had a problem with my kidneys. It looked like I was in end stage kidney failure, but they weren't sure if it was permanent. I was in shock, and I think my dad was in shock as well.

I can't remember much about that first day, apart from the fact that part of me was relieved. Another part of me was angry at the first doctor for diagnosing a sprained ankle when my health issue had nothing to do with a sprain.

The main problem at that point was that I was not passing any urine. I was just retaining fluid. The toxins in my blood were very high. They decided the one way to bring the toxins down quickly was to put me on peritoneal dialysis.

In those days, peritoneal dialysis was quite primitive. They inserted a hard plastic cannula, or tube, into my peritoneum. The peritoneum is a membrane that lines the walls of the abdominal and pelvic cavities in the human torso. In dialysis of this kind, the cavities are filled with a liquid that draws toxins and waste products through the membrane, so they can be removed. I was not entirely clear about the process. The urea and creatinine building up in my body were probably impacting my thinking.

My first peritoneal treatment went on overnight. The worst part was when the fluid was removed from my peritoneum. They used a small pump to suck on the inside of my abdomen, which was very painful. These days peritoneal dialysis is a very gentle treatment used by a large number of dialysis patients as part of their normal regime.

The one thing that was still working for me was my appreciation of attractive women, especially nurses, and there were a few. The nurses seemed to enjoy looking after me, which I didn't mind at all.

After more tests and probably a week or so of dialysis treatments, the doctors had enough information to confirm what was wrong with me. I expected good news. There was another young bloke in the same ward who had come in with end stage renal failure as well, and they had just told him that it was only temporary. He was going to be fine. In my head, that was the way it was going to pan out for me as well.

When the doctors came in to tell me and my dad the results of the examinations, they basically said that my kidneys had shrunk, which they believed was due to what they called 'reflux neuropathy'. That was the cause of my end stage renal failure. They couldn't understand how I had not come in earlier – my blood results were extremely toxic, and any normal person would have been dead. So in one sense I was lucky.

I thought they could do something to increase my kidney function, and I would be fine like the other young guy in the ward. But it wasn't meant to be for me. It could have been a scene from *Star Trek*, but sci-fi did not come to my rescue. On the positive side, though, the other young guy really was fine.

After they confirmed that I had no way of living my life without some form of dialysis or a kidney transplant, our family had a lot of things to consider. Mum and Lin returned from South Africa, my brother Josh came back from Penang, and Luke returned from where he was working in Fiji.

This was one of the most emotional times that I can recall in my life. My whole family was there to support me, and I didn't feel so alone.

I really liked music when I was 17, and my favourite musician was James Taylor. Josh brought me a James Taylor tape from his travels in Penang. It had the song 'You've Got a Friend' on it. I remember lying in bed, listening to it over and over again, during the lead-up to the doctors telling me about my options. I used to just cry because I was so worried, but I was also happy that I wasn't alone.

Each member of my family offered to provide a kidney for a transplant. But I felt that I was still young and tough, so I could handle a short period on dialysis. I felt I would get a transplant without too much of a problem. I also didn't want to affect their lives. So I decided to go on dialysis.

As part of that process, the nurses showed me what dialysis actually meant. The first thing they showed me was what the dialysis machines were, then how dialysis worked. For a 17-year-old, walking into the dialysis ward at Royal Prince Alfred was like walking into some torture chamber. But the nurses were fantastic and very caring.

It was a huge shock to me that everyone else on dialysis was old and I was only 17. It made me feel very uncomfortable. I don't know why. Maybe I felt that I was just too young and kidney failure was for old people. As the years went by, I met many more young people who were on dialysis.

My First Year on Dialysis

Haemodialysis was a more effective routine treatment than peritoneal dialysis in 1978. I chose haemodialysis. A surgeon had to operate on the veins in my arms so that I could be hooked up properly to the machines. I had two fistulas inserted, one in the right wrist and one in the left. The right fistula was external, meaning two plastic tubes were joined internally to a vein and an artery, then brought through the skin near the wrist to be joined to the machines externally. I could dialyse using the external fistula exclusively until the internal, or AV, fistula on the left was working. The fistulas enabled the blood to get out of my body, circulate through the dialyser, and return to my body. Eventually I would learn how to insert needles into the veins in my left arm for a less exposed dialysis circuit, but the fistula there needed to mature for a few months before I could use it.

I spent the rest of 1978 in hospital, getting better and trying to convince my mum and dad that things would be OK. I am sure it was very difficult for all my family to handle that I was on dialysis and things might not be as normal as they used to be.

I think the hardest time for my family was Christmas 1978, but I can't remember what we did that year. I was still very sick. I don't think I got a pass out of hospital for the holiday.

The surgeon eventually removed the external fistula when the nurses could switch me to using the internal fistula. Initially, that process was the most painful thing I had ever felt. I needed to have local anaesthetic injected into the skin before inserting the dialysis needles. That made me feel that I was not going to be able to do it myself. The needles were 14- or 15-gauge (about one-eighth of an inch) in diameter and were over an inch long.

I needed to focus. I was determined that I was going to have a life outside the hospital. It was what I wanted most, and the only way to get it was to dialyse myself at home. I told the doctors that I would like to go home on dialysis but I would need my mum to help me. Mum agreed eventually, and I was trained how to insert the needles, maintain the machine, and dialyse over the following two to three months.

Before the medical staff would agree to let me dialyse at home, they needed to confirm that I was capable from a psychological perspective. I spoke to the team psychiatrist, to determine if I was at risk to kill myself. There had been incidents overseas in which patients had killed themselves via their dialysis machines when they got home, because they didn't want to be kept alive by machines.

My session went well. At the beginning, I said that I had one question to ask him at the end. He agreed. The psychiatrist was a very easy-going character; I guess he needed to be that way because of his occupation.

At the end of the session, he said, 'So what was that question you wanted to ask me?'

I said, 'Well, what do you reckon – am I crazy or not?'

He smiled and said, 'You're just as same as I am, Phil.'

From that point forward, I felt at ease with the psychiatrist.

It was good having him as part of the treatment team, because it was not easy dealing with dialysis at 17, let alone dealing with my parents. Though I loved them with all my heart, I could not discuss some things with them. I used sessions with the psychiatrist like counselling sessions to deal with issues like convincing Mum and Dad that things would be all right and they shouldn't worry about me so much. I knew it was natural for them to be concerned, and I did appreciate the concern, but sometimes they were too much.

The most important things to me were that I wanted to live as normal a life as I could, and I did not want to have a negative impact my family. I was glad that I was the one going through this and not one of my siblings. The James Taylor song 'You've Got a Friend' hit home then and now. My brothers and sister were there for me, and are still my best friends.

Even though my family probably couldn't believe this was happening to one of us, I felt that I would survive and could handle what was coming my way, at least for a short period. Unfortunately, it ended up being a lot longer than any of us imagined.

I know it was very hard for Mum and Dad to accept that I was on dialysis. They didn't really know, initially, how to help me. My relationship with them had to be open enough for me to be totally honest with them. Sometimes it was hard, but we got there in the end. I think they eventually realised I needed to be free to make my own decisions. I knew I could always count on them to give me their opinions, which was fine, but it took some time for them to understood that I needed to be in control of my own life.

Dialysis for young people was not very common when I started. Most patients were older and had experienced renal failure due to overuse of pain killers. I think my case may have been an eye-opener for that renal unit that dialysis was not just an old people's problem any more.

There may be young people going through similar struggles as they read this book. I hope my story helps you understand that your life has not ended. There are ways to have a good life with kidney failure, given support from family and friends.

2

Finding a Balance: The First Year at Home

Learning to put needles in to myself was probably the hardest, strangest experience I have ever had. I knew I had to do it if I was going to have any sort of life, but each time I knew I would inflict pain on myself. I felt as if I was punishing myself for some reason. It took a lot of patience from the nurses. I would shake when I handled the needles. On many occasions, I missed the vein on the first try and had to do it again. If I couldn't face it, one of the nurses had to put the needles in for me.

At some points, I thought I was never going to be able to do it. But eventually I got better and didn't 'bomb' myself. That was the term for getting the needle into the vein and going straight through the other side of the vein, which was very painful. Hirudoid cream, used to get rid of bruising, was my best friend for many months.

My training included how to use the dialysis machine and what to do if something went wrong while I was on dialysis. The next step was to bring Mum on board, because Mum was going to need to learn the basics to help me if I got into trouble. I was nervous about this at first. No matter how much I loved her and knew she would do everything she could to help, I felt dialysis was my responsibility.

Mum did her best to learn and was always there to help – but she never learned how to put in the needles. By the time I went home, I preferred to do it myself anyway. I was getting pretty good at it.

One of the main problems that could occur was bombing myself and having to find another site to put the needles in. If I couldn't find a site, I had to go into hospital. I could not be without dialysis for more than two days, as the toxins and fluid in my body would build up to a point that would make me very sick. I wanted to stay out of hospital as much as I could.

The other main problem was passing out in mid-treatment because of low blood pressure. I had to come off dialysis before I passed out or I could potentially kick the bucket. Identifying the feeling of impending unconsciousness was very important. I needed to have confidence in my ability to recognise the signal and start the process of coming off the machine, with Mum's help.

The best way to describe this feeling is that it's similar to the feeling one has when given a sedative. The medical staff tell you to count back from ten. Most of us never get that far, but have experienced the shaky sensation that kicks in around number nine. That's the signal. The trick is *not* to get to the point of passing out, which in my experience happens around number seven. You don't have much time.

After being on dialysis at home for a few months, I became quite independent. My relationship with my parents went through many changes during those initial months. I became more up front with Mum and Dad, and they found it hard to get used to this part of being on dialysis. Previously, I had done what I was told and followed the line. That was no longer the case. It took them quite some time to realise that I needed to do this for myself. I think this adjustment made my relationship with Mum and Dad a lot better in the end, but it was hard initially. My brothers and sister also had a bit of trouble understanding.

We were lucky enough to have an area in our rented house where the dialysis machine could be installed. By the time I was ready to leave the hospital, the machine and supplies were all set up and ready for me.

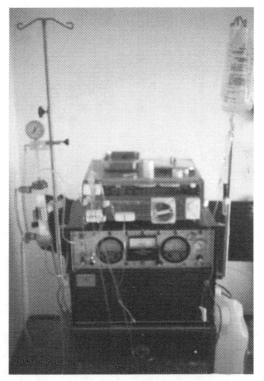

The Dialysis Machine

From the time I first went into hospital to the point when I came home was about eight months – a long time being away from friends, family, and the rest of my life. It was time for me to figure out what I was going to do now.

One of the first things to do was to see if I could get back to school and catch up. I was lucky: the school I attended, Cumberland High School, gave me an assessment so that I could move to my final year. But it wasn't going to be easy catching up on all the material I had missed. I was finding that I couldn't concentrate very well, and I had trouble remembering things. I used study guides to help me, but I knew I wouldn't do very well.

My last year in high school, 1979, was also the year I had planned to get my driver's license. With everything else that was going on in my life, I managed to pass my driving test. I bought my first car, a Ford Anglia.

I seemed to have more time to do things after my hospital stint. My friends didn't come over to visit me on dialysis – it wasn't the best environment, and for them it was probably very foreign and potentially scary.

My brothers and sister were supportive. They tried to include me in what they did. I was quite good at playing guitar, and I used to go and see my brothers, Luke and Pearse, perform most weekends in a local pub, Hero of Waterloo. I would play one or two songs with them occasionally, and they eventually let me work with them every Saturday night. That improved my social life significantly.

I hung out with my school friends during the week but not on weekends, except for the occasional times when Glen and Wayne came to see me play. I enjoyed those times with Luke and Pearse so much. We had some interesting after-gig parties. I also got on well with most of their friends, which was an added bonus.

When I worked with Pearse and Luke, I drove my mum's car to where Pearse lived at Lane Cove and stayed overnight with him. I met some wonderful people during these times and some gorgeous women.

One night when we were playing at the Hero of Waterloo, a woman I had met was there as usual. She came to see us play most weekends with her friend. She was older than me, I would guess close to 30. I was into older women in those days. She was blonde with blue eyes and very attractive. We became very close over a period of time, enjoying each other's company and having a good laugh at the pub.

On that night, I gave her a lift back to her place. I won't forget what followed. It was my first time, and I hadn't realised how much I was missing. She was an amazing woman, and we had a fantastic night – but no one knew where I was.

In those days there weren't mobile phones. You couldn't just text to say 'I am running late and will be back home soon'. Instead you had to use a landline or, in my case, a call box at the end of the road. I did try to let Pearse know that I was fine and staying over with a friend, but no one answered his phone. I tried again a little bit later. By the time I got through to Pearse, it was early in the morning, and he had already rung Mum and Dad to see if I had gone home.

As you can imagine, my parents were not impressed at all when I rang them. They were in the process of calling the police. My dad could have killed me, or at least that's how he sounded on the phone. It was the only time I ever had to say goodbye to a woman in the morning and go back home to my parents: very embarrassing.

I never spoke to my parents about it, but they seemed a lot more relaxed about me going out after that. I continued to see the woman for a while, but it wasn't anything serious or long-term.

My last year in high school was pretty amazing. The fact that I was dialysing every two days during the week (Monday, Wednesday, and Friday) was fantastic because I always had weekends off. Dialysis started to become part of my life. I realised that life wasn't going to be that bad. I was very glad to be alive, even on dialysis.

I was introduced to many great musicians and jammed with them at parties. My brothers and I went to different bars. Once I was 18, I was legal to drink, but I never drank a lot because of the fluid restriction I was on: 800 millilitres per day.

I tended to drink whisky or dark rum with Coke because those drinks had less fluid than beer, but occasionally I had a lime and soda when I was sweating, as the pubs were very hot in those days. It was a bit like of a sauna onstage, and I knew I could drink more. Nevertheless, I tended to gain anywhere from three to five kilos between dialysis sessions, indicating that my fluid intake routinely was more than my body could handle. But I was alive and well and having a great time. I was always able to take the weight off during dialysis. The weather in summer helped to keep my weight down as well because I perspired a lot.

One of the places that Luke and Pearse took me was the All Nations Club, which was in Kings Cross. It was an amazing place were all the musos went after their gigs and partied until the early hours. On one occasion, Tommy Emmanuel was there. We talked while listening to the Night & Day band. Billy Day, the band leader, asked me if I wanted to get up and do a song.

As I got to the stage, I thought Billy was handing me a guitar, but Tommy was behind me and Billy had meant to give the guitar to Tommy. When I realised what had happened, I turned around to Tommy. He said, 'That's fine, Phil. You play guitar; I'll play the drums.'

I will never forget that night. It was one of my best nights at the All Nations Club. I wonder if Tommy even remembers that night? Probably not – it was a long time ago. The thing is, Tommy is a fantastic guitarist and also an amazing drummer. He is an amazing talent. I was glad to know him at that time of my life.

During that last year of high school, I had to decide what I wanted to do. Of course my parents wanted me to get a job and not be a musician. Before dialysis, I had planned to join one of the forces, probably the air force, and become an officer. That was no longer possible. My friends were starting to get into computers. I would have liked to do that as well, but I never got high enough grades to get into university. I missed it by one point.

Unfortunately, I wasn't good enough to play in pubs on my own. I knew in my heart of hearts that gigging in pubs would not really be the way forward for me anyway. I needed a bit of security in my life, and a day job would give me focus and a regular income. I also saw how hard my brothers worked, and I didn't have a lot of time or, more importantly, confidence in my ability to do what they did.

When I graduated high school, we had the standard farewell. By that point I had bought another car, a Ford Falcon, a beast with a lot of power. It was a column shift and built like a tank. Even though I spent a lot of my weekends with my brothers, I did also have some great friends at school. Wayne and Glen stick out in my mind the most. They each ended up going to university and becoming very successful in the computer industry. Wayne married the girl he dated in school, and they had a couple of children. Glen went down a similar route and is now married with two children.

Glen and Wayne came to see me play a few times on the weekends, but most of the people at school had no idea what I did. I sort of liked it that way. We had a great high school graduation, and everyone I knew moved into careers that suited their talents. They've generally done well for themselves.

That first year or so that I was on dialysis was pretty amazing. I feel privileged to have experienced those fine times with my brothers and the people I met. I believe those experiences helped me focus on what I wanted and gave me an outlet to deal with dialysis and to stay positive.

The thing that helped me the most was finding a way to balance my relationship with my parents. My parents had to understand that I needed my freedom. I wasn't sure how long I would around, especially in those early days on dialysis. Establishing this point helped my relationship with them over the years. I have always tried to be straight with them.

Finding the balance with my parents helped me find balance in my life. Being realistic and honest about my feelings helped us all realise I needed a balance of work and play in my life. I needed to do dialysis and go to school, and playing music balanced those obligations.

There is a balance in life that we all need to find. I don't just mean work-life balance. I mean the balance between positive and negative thoughts or feelings. In those early days on dialysis, I saw both the good and bad sides. I had to work out how to deal with all those thoughts. I found the best way to deal with the negative feelings was to accept the situation, after confirming that there was no other option. Then I sought the positive feelings in the situation – or, as they say, 'looked for the silver lining'.

An example of this was that each time I had to go on the machine, I was petrified of not being able to put in my needles properly. I knew that my mother couldn't do it. Sometimes the fear, frustration, and anger were overpowering, especially if I'd had a bad day.

The way I tried to turn these feelings around was to focus on how I felt when I was performing on the weekends. I needed to dialyse to perform. That gave me the boost that I needed, most of the time, to focus and put in the needles.

I know there are times when challenging situations arise in people's lives. You can either look at them as positive or negative, depending on how you feel at the time. I believe you need to find a way to deal with all feelings, good and bad, for themselves. Learn how to deal with these challenges; otherwise they will overpower you. I speak from personal experience.

There is nothing wrong with feeling negative occasionally. Without understanding how to handle negative feelings, you will not be able to handle the times when negative thoughts try to take over your life. You need to be able to restore a balanced viewpoint so that you can handle the bad times as well as the good.

If you get to a point where the balance in your life is lost and your focus is always negative, identify a positive activity that gives you enjoyment, I found music has helped me in this way. When you have found this activity, you can refocus your energies and rebalance your life.

Over the thirty-seven years that I have been on dialysis and dealing with transplants, I have been in situations where I was not able to rebalance my life. During these times, I have asked for medical advice and looked at complementary therapies (e.g., meditation and relaxation). Apart from advice from my doctors, I have found that the complementary therapies have helped me considerably throughout the challenges.

Sometimes things are not in your control. Understanding that medical advice and complementary therapy may help you find the balance is important. I believe that a combination of different therapies helps, not necessarily just one approach. Again, it comes down to a balance and your personal choice.

Most people don't want to go straight onto medication if they are having trouble handling life. I don't believe medication is the answer in every case. You should always have the opportunity to decide what is right for you in consultation with medical practitioners and therapists.

You may have gathered that I have experienced anxiety and depression along the way. I have looked at different avenues to help me. I have found that a balance of medical advice, complementary therapies, and the support of family and friends have helped considerably I have also found that I handle stress a lot better when I include music as part of the balance.

3

The First

In December 1979, I was introduced to one of the side effects of dialysis and kidney failure: hyperparathyroidism. The doctors discovered that I had a large amount of calcium in my blood, and my phosphate levels were high. My bone density was low and I was getting skeletal pain. This led to the conclusion that I had a problem with my parathyroids.

The parathyroids control the levels of calcium in the blood. When they are overactive, they tend to draw calcium from the bones. This was what was happening to me. My bones could have become very brittle if the doctors hadn't fixed the problem with the parathyroids.

The doctors confirmed the diagnosis by doing a bone biopsy, taking a piece of bone from my hip. They put the piece of bone under a microscope to see whether the calcium in it was depleted. It was, so they booked me in for a parathyroidectomy to remove my parathyroids. After my parathyroids were removed, the excess calcium in my blood was drawn straight back into my bones.

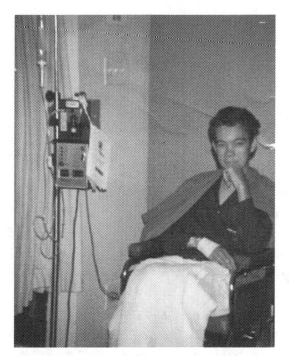

Calcium drip post operation

I had an intravenous calcium drip for several days until the calcium level stabilised in my blood. I was discharged on Christmas Eve 1979.

The new year held a whole new set of surprises for me. To be honest, I don't think I was ready for what was going to happen next.

The year started off with me looking at what types of jobs I could do so that I could dialyse every second day. Most of those jobs were in clerical work. Unfortunately, employers rejected me because I was on dialysis. They said I would not pass their medical assessments because of my kidney failure. I felt pretty low about my employment prospects, so I decided to apply to a technical college and do a course.

As I really enjoyed photography, I applied for a course in photography at Meadowbank Technical College. I went into the college for the enrolment day, and it turned out that there were no more places left for the photography course. The course advisor suggested that I could still do the photography as part of an arts diploma.

My only problem with that was that I wasn't the artist in the family. That was Josh. Still, the course advisor convinced me to apply and asked if I had any drawings to show her. Obviously, I hadn't. She said that I had to draw something, and I should follow her.

She took me into a studio and arranged a large table with a couple of small tables on top. She then placed a sheet over them. To my surprise, she produced an animal skull from a cupboard and asked me to sketch it. I spent the next half an hour trying to make the sketch look something like the skull on the table.

When I was finished, she came back and asked me a few questions. She said she was impressed with the sketch and couldn't believe I had never done art before. I couldn't believe it either. I had just passed the entry to the art diploma. Happy days! I now had something to do with my life.

After a couple of months, though, I found that the costs associated with the course were going to make it impossible for me to continue. To be honest, I wasn't really into modern art, which was a lot of what they were teaching. So I left the course. I felt that I could always go back and do the photography when I was able to afford it.

On April 1, I got a call from the hospital. They had a kidney available for transplantation from a cadaver donation. At first I thought it was an April Fool's joke, but I soon realised it wasn't.

As this was my first kidney transplant, I was full of excitement as well as trepidation. I had no idea what to expect. When you are dialysing three times a week for six hours a time, you don't have a lot of opportunity to understand what having a new kidney would be like – or at least I certainly didn't. I think my family was excited for me but also nervous about the proposition that their son and brother was about to go in for a very long operation.

Back in 1980, kidney transplantation techniques had become standardized, and they followed the same protocols for all patients. Compared to modern transplants, these protocols would probably be considered backward, but the doctors did what they needed to do to achieve the end goal: provide an opportunity for a dialysis patient to live a normal life off dialysis.

The transplant kidney was in good condition and considered a perfect match for me, according to the technologies they had available then.

When I went into the transplant ward, my skin had to be sterilised. I had a shower in the most pungent ointment. It made me feel like I had just been washing in iodine and some rainwater that had been sitting in grass clippings for two weeks – not nice. After this experience I was shaved from nipple to kneecap, which again for me was something that did not settle very well, especially when I was told that they needed to re-shave my groin. (The things that stick in my mind after all these years!)

The kidney was transplanted on my right side, in my lower abdomen. This was so they could get access to my bladder, to connect the ureters, and to the main arteries, for the blood flow. The operations took about eight hours in those days, as compared to about three hours with today's techniques. After the operation, I was in a lot of pain. I was also on dialysis, which for me wasn't a great sign.

After I completed the dialysis, the nurses made me walk around with one nurse on either side. I can't remember if this was straight away or maybe the next day. I do know that it hurt.

The worst part was that the kidney wasn't working. The nurses were great; they supported me a lot through that first transplant.

I had to go for tests, biopsies, and all sorts of poking and prodding to see what was happening inside.

It turned out that I had what is called a 'sleeping kidney', where there doesn't appear to be organ rejection, but the kidney is just not working. My family tried to remain positive, but it was hard for them and me.

The transplant ward at that time was towards the back of the Royal Prince Alfred Hospital. There was only one entrance, which had blue lights that they used to disinfect anything that came in. The main ward had three beds for patients whose kidneys were working. Patients stayed there just for the final days before they went home. There were also several individual care rooms, each with one bed.

I was in an individual care room when I first went into the transplant unit. I must have been in it for a couple of weeks. There was a lot of discussion about why the kidney wasn't working, and they tried to figure out what would give it a kick start. They tried not to dialyse me too much, as that was drying me out, and they thought that might be why the transplant wasn't working.

I was eventually moved to the main ward, which was a bit better. At least I could see the daylight. The main problem with the transplant ward was that I could not see family or friends. The only way to communicate with them was via a phone intercom connected to a wall just outside the ward. The isolation was the worst part about the process. Because I was in there for a considerable length of time, it really did my head in.

The occupational health people tried to find me things to do. I ended up making teddy bears, would you believe. It was like I was in a psychiatric ward in one of those old black-and-white horror movies – or at least that's what I thought it would have been like.

As things were starting to get to me, I was allowed to get my guitar, after it was zapped by the blue light to disinfect it. Then I could play music in the ward, to keep myself from going bonkers. Days and weeks went by with more tests, more injections, and still no working kidney.

I started to get symptoms of chemical diabetes, brought on by one of the drugs. This seemed to resolve itself when they changed my medication. The transplant also highlighted a change in my liver function, which they thought might be a result of exposure to hepatitis. I now have antibodies for hepatitis C, but it is not active. Doctors continue check my liver function, but they believe the hep C will not come back.

One of the worst times I had in this transplant was when I was put on a drug to make me relax. I had an opposite reaction: it gave me muscle spasms in my neck. This went on for at least eight hours. They tested my blood to identify what the issue was, and eventually had to give me another drug to counteract the effect. For those eight hours, I really thought that someone was trying to break my neck, and I couldn't stop it from happening. It was probably the scariest experience I have had in all my transplants.

The whole experience was nerve-racking, emotional, depressing, and crazy. By the time they eventually took the transplant out, I was totally drained. I hate to say it, but I was reluctant to go for another one.

After coming out of hospital, I developed acute appendicitis. That meant I had to go back in and have my appendix removed. We have since felt that the appendicitis had something to do with why the kidney didn't work, but we will never really know.

In the whole scheme of things, I learnt that I needed to have faith in the people who were looking after me. I also realised that there were things in my control and things not in my control. I needed to relax, stay positive, and look for the silver lining.

Without the experience of this transplant, I would never have discovered relaxation or meditation. I started doing this type of therapy on the ward and continued it afterwards, learning different techniques. Today, I don't use it very often, but when I feel things getting on top of me, I do follow the relaxation techniques I learned. Over the last few years I have joined a Buddhist Thai temple to learn more about meditation, which I also use to help me focus on the positives.

A balanced view is very important when you go through life challenges. Relaxation and meditation, I believe, can help you deal with many day-to-day challenges and keep your focus on the positive.

4

Work

After I had recovered from the transplant and things settles down, I registered for unemployment benefits. I didn't stay on them long, as I was very focused on getting a job.

I found a temporary job as an accounts clerk in the New South Wales Housing Association for twelve months. The job was available because a woman was on maternity leave. It was a great break for me. I needed some income, and I didn't want to be on benefit. I also thought that I could go back to photography part-time.

The people I worked with were fantastic and quite an eclectic group. I learnt several things while I was there, apart from accounting practices, including how to play card games like 21, 500. It was also my first introduction to the arcade games Space Invaders and Asteroids, and to long pub lunches. Working was a great confidence boost. I had my independence, and the people I worked with were great fun. There was certainly no office politics to worry about in those days.

I was very lucky that the job gave me an opportunity to look at a career in public service, which suited me fine. I was still doing the occasional gig with Luke and Pearse on weekends as well. I decided not to do the photography course, as it was an expensive pastime. I preferred saving the money and playing with Pearse and Luke.

By the time the temporary job came to an end in late 1981, I had already applied for positions in the Commonwealth Public Service as a clerical assistant and clerk. I was lucky enough to get a clerical assistant role right away and started working in the Australian Taxation Office, in the sales tax area.

My main task was to search for files in the tax office at Parramatta. I was also given the essential task of making tea for all the tax assessors at ten o'clock and three o'clock every day, which I didn't mind. It gave my day a bit of structure. According to the assessors, nothing was more important than making the tea, so I planned my days around that task. Of course I knew that they were just kidding. I was new to the public service, and this was a gentle sort of initiation.

As I did such a good job making tea, and was the only bloke who had ever done it, the tax assessors gave me a present when I was eventually promoted to clerk. The present was a voucher for a music compact disc, a brand-new technology at the time.

My promotion to sales tax assessment clerk was my first introduction to office politics. The other clerical assistants were not happy that I got promoted. It had always been my plan to get my first job, do a good job at it, and work my way up. I was doing that. I had originally applied for public service employment via both the clerical assistant and clerk tests, and I had passed both. I was fully qualified to take on the clerk's role when a job became available.

Unfortunately, some of my former colleagues had a problem with this situation. I think they were happy for me, and we still hung out together. But they felt I had taken a shortcut, which I hadn't. Soon after this, the public service changed its structure to a single stream of clerical positions, which was a lot more sensible.

I always tried to avoid the politics, laugh it off. I preferred to be a diplomat to get what I wanted. I found that this approach was a useful way to get the job done and avoid the politics. Sometimes, however, there were pathological colleagues who were willing to use others or a situation to get noticed or deflect criticism. I was never one to behave like that. However, I have learnt that the more aggressive people who do play politics are often in the top jobs in any line of work, private or public.

The Commonwealth Public Service was very understanding about my dialysis and my condition. I was employed in 1981, the United Nation's International Year of Disabled Persons, which gave me insight as to what that initiative was all about. Most people that were identified as disabled were people who had visible disabilities, such as being confined to a wheelchair. I was asked to get involved with the public service disability liaison group because I was in a different category.

One of the hardest things I found to understand was other people's perceptions of disability – that is, their opinion as to whether a person was disabled or not. I found it difficult to get the group to understand that disability should be considered on the basis on how a condition impacted a person's quality of life. I was disabled to a degree. My disability was real but limited. I had a reasonable quality of life, mainly due to my friends' and family's support. I was independent enough to live my own life and not have the dialysis define me.

But people on dialysis have limits on what they can do, and I wanted the committee to realise that. If dialysis does not go well, the person on dialysis should not be penalised for not being able to get into work.

I wasn't able to keep up with the committee due to work commitments and dialysis. But I believe that the International Year of Disabled Persons was one of the first times that people with disabilities were able to have a say in their futures. I believe things have changed for the better in many places, and I hope this continues.

I admit that in the early days of my employment with the public service, I tried to avoid being considered disabled. I just wanted to be treated like any other person. I was lucky at that point to be able to work full-time flexible hours while maintaining dialysis. I know things have changed considerably, but in those days it was still very early in the development of the Disability Discrimination Act, and such accommodation was not the norm.

I worked full-time for most of my employment in the public service, and I believe I did very well considering the circumstances in my life. I appreciate the public service taking me on when no one else would after I left school. Without their support, I would never have achieved what I have been able to in my life.

The best thing that came out of 1981 was that I learnt not to give up, no matter what. I learnt to strive for my goals: a career, independence, and a normal quality of life (or what I thought was normal at that time). My family was instrumental in keeping me focused on what I wanted, and I am very grateful for their persistence. I had achieved a lot since making that first cup of tea for the sales tax assessors.

The other thing I realised was that, no matter how much I wanted to be a musician, I needed to be employed in regular work to achieve that aim. The route of becoming a public servant enabled me to do my music and have an income to enjoy the rest of my life. I could never have moved to London to work without setting goals and taking the opportunities I got during my public service career.

5

The Second

After I had been at the sales tax office for a year or so, my parents looked at buying a new house in Windsor, New South Wales. It had space for a separate home dialysis room. That was great, but it also looked like I would be doing home dialysis for the rest of my life. I was starting to feel trapped. Something had to change. I was still living at home with my parents, and I realised that I couldn't live at home anymore.

After getting my promotion, I found that I wanted to try different things. I started learning, would you believe, jazz dancing. I took lessons at a little studio on the other side of the railway station from the tax office, which was in Church Street. I had always wanted to be in musicals and thought I could become the next Fred Astaire. I was still playing with my brothers when I could, but I wanted to try something different, and the dancing certainly managed that for me.

It was a fact of life with me that when things were going well, something else would come from left field and give me another challenge. That was exactly what happened at this point. I got a call from the hospital to confirm that they had another kidney available for transplant – another perfect match.

During this transplant, I kept a diary, which I quote from below. The transplant took place on 18 January 1982, and the organ came from a cadaver donor. As with the previous attempt, this new kidney did not start to work immediately.

***

Thursday, 21 January 1982

Well, here I am, waiting for another dialysis. Hopefully it will be the last for a while. Since I've been in hospital, I've been feeling pretty weak, but I guess that's expected. Sometimes my eyesight goes a bit blurred, but that's getting better.

I used the pan today, and I think that made me feel a bit better. I really want this kidney to work. I feel that it will, crossed fingers. I really hope it will.

Wednesday, 27 January 1982

This was my second week in, and I've had a few problems. They had to take a haematoma out (i.e., blood clot) and that was a relief. They took it out Monday, and I was really sore. Today I'm not feeling too bad. I'm just worried about the kidney. I really want it to work, but I'm tired. They had to put in two more drains because of the blood clot, and they're irritating a bit. I guess that is expected.

I seem to be complaining a lot these days, but I just want the kidney to work, and I know it will!

On a good note, I'm passing wind and a little bit of bloody urine. I hope that's the start for the better. I got dialysed yesterday, and with a bit of luck I will only need to be dialysed tomorrow. We got a new transplant patient today, so the nurses are pretty busy.

Friday, 29 January 1982

A new day and I feel good, but the kidney isn't producing anything much. I guess we can only hope. The little bit of urine that I passed this morning (5–10 mls) wasn't as bloodstained as the previous, but I just wish it was a lot more urine.

Dr Chess has been in about twenty minutes ago. He says that the kidney is still sleeping, which means that the kidney is not producing urine. But it does not appear to be rejecting and is well perfused, which means the kidney has enough blood circulating. I went for an ultrasound at about 10 a.m. and no results have come back yet. I have to wait. No news is good news. I used to get on really well with Dr Chess. He used to bring in a chessboard when he wasn't on shift, and we would play chess. He knew that I got bored very easily.

One thing I liked about this transplant is that I seem to feel more relaxed about it, not so uptight. The reason for this is that I have been able to talk to Mum and Dad a lot more about the way I feel, not holding back as much as last time. I must admit I miss them and the rest of the clan! When the kidney works, I am going to be so happy. Boy, when that happens, what a party.

There is always a possibility that the kidney won't work. *But,* with help from the guy upstairs and faith in the doctors and myself, I reckon this one will work, even if it takes as long as the other did *not* to work,

This one will work!

Later that day:

Dr Rudder came in earlier today and confirmed that the kidney was well perfused with blood, so things are looking good. Just no urine, or at least, not a lot. Overall, I feel good tonight (this is at 10 p.m.). I'm watching *Steptoe and Son.*

It's going to be a long weekend tomorrow. I don't know when I will have another dialysis, but I hope I won't need one! I am enjoying a really nice cup of tea the new nurse made for me. She's English, very pretty, and she has a twin sister who is a nurse on the dialysis ward. If only I had enough energy to chase them around the ward. It is quite funny when you see one, then later on the other pops in to say hello. It does get confusing, making sure I keep track of what I say to one nurse or the other.

Saturday, 30 January 1982

Well, it was my last drip for rejection for a while. The needle went into the tissue, so they had to put a new needle in, which I didn't appreciate. My veins are not that great at the moment, and I feel a bit like a pincushion. The drip has been out now since 5 p.m., and I feel more relaxed after having another half cup of tea. [NB: even though I'd had a transplant, I was still on a fluid restriction of 800 mls.]

The left drain is still draining quite a bit, but the right one is slowing right down, so they may take it out soon. [The reason for two drains is that one goes above and one below the kidney to make sure blood does not build up in the cavity where the kidney is deposited.]

Some really good news is that tonight, after coming off the drip and eating something, I passed 35 mls of urine in one go. So maybe the kidney is starting. Only time will tell. God, but I'm hopeful and have faith. Anyway, we can only wait and see. I will go on dialysis on Monday, so I'll have a whole day to relax and have a good sleep tonight.

Sunday, 31 January 1982

Today has been a bit boring. The weather was dull and raining, so I felt a bit down. I felt like I was stuck in one place and not making progress. But I am really, as I'm producing more urine and it's clear. I think I may be missing my family and seeing my friends, etc. I may get Mum to get Jonno and Glen's phone number so I can call them.

Tuesday, 2 February 1982

Well! What a day!

Started off with me thinking I was going to get another blood leak (haematoma) because the doctors were going to do a biopsy on the kidney to see if it was working, to the end of the day where I am sitting here just writing in my diary and the biopsy has been called off. The professor wants to give the kidney a rest from the last bleed and let it heal a bit more. Boy, am I relieved. I was worried, as I told Mum and Dad, that everything was happening too quickly for me. I was getting nervous, but now that they have delayed a few things for a while, I can gather my thoughts a bit better.

I might try to help one of the other transplant patients. She's a frail old girl, and as she is going through this at her age, she's a bit scared. Basically she is having a biopsy tomorrow, and I hope they go well for her. I did tell her that it doesn't hurt. I have already had one from the previous transplant. I think the way they were changing their minds today with me made her nervous, and she did have a lot of questions. I hope I was able to help. I did say that I felt she should talk to the head sister or the doctors tomorrow, when they see her before she has the biopsy (if she does).

Other than that I got the drain out today. It feels strange, but I am sure a good night's sleep will help. Still have got good hopes that I give it (the kidney) a fair go. I'm thinking of all of my family while I'm in here. I love them all. I hope, with the help of the guy upstairs and my faith and the faith of all the *wonderful* people that love me, I'll make it right to the other end of the transplant ward and *home*!

(I know I may be sounding a bit religious these days, but I have a chat to the guy upstairs. That helps sometimes when you can't talk about everything to family. I try not to bother him too much.

***

[The conversations I used to have, and occasionally still do, with the guy upstairs helped me feel not so alone in the isolation ward. It was very lonely, even though I did get on very well with the nurses. Sometimes I felt better talking over something that was on my mind with the guy upstairs. I never really got a reply, but it helped me clarify my thoughts and helped me deal with the isolated conditions.]

***

Wednesday, 3 February 1982

A new day, but I didn't do much apart from cry. I think the kidney is coming good, but I won't really know until a biopsy is done on Friday. I'm tired and nervous about the kidney, but I've got to calm down and just let it happen, if it does. If not, then have another go, but a long time off for me at this point.

I'd like to go on holiday if this one's not the one. Just get *my* life in order and come back in a year or so. Do dialysis again in Sydney after I've seen a bit of the world. I suppose I'd be content to wait for another kidney transplant. I think this would be the last one for a while, but I can't say for sure, because how could you refuse a chance to live a happy, normal, everyday life, not sure that the next kidney might be the one that worked? I am still hoping that this kidney works, as it's got good perfusion. Now that my drain is out, I feel a lot better.

I didn't take the mogadon [an old-fashioned sleeping tablet] tonight because I want to see if I can sleep without one. I hope so because when I leave here I want to be able to pass urine, sleep, and drink and eat what I want. Maybe with some luck the kidney could last me for the rest of my life. Dear Lord, when you see the donor, please say that I will do my best to keep his or her kidney safe and well. The basic problem is that no matter what way I want it to be,

I can't stop the kidney from rejecting me. I can only hope that the guy upstairs is on my side this time.

Please!

Summary from doctors today – good perfusion, better than the first scan, so I am hopeful and a little less nervous.

Tomorrow, Thursday, the biopsy!

Well, who can say what will happen? Won't really know until the Monday, anyway.

I think my next entry may be my last until I hear about my biopsy results. I'd better get some rest for the biopsy tomorrow, so …

Goodnight!

And

Relax.

Thursday, 4 February 1982

The biopsy was today. They took two pieces of kidney, as apparently there looks like a bit of rejection but hopefully not much. They've given me a big dose of anti-rejection drug to see if this will correct it. I think the kidney will be good, but I can only hope. I'd really like to wait until Monday when the real results will be known, but I'm glad that they caught this rejection and hope the treatment works. The biopsy itself was quite good. My relaxation therapy came in handy again, so it didn't hurt.

We can only really tell if the kidney is working by the toxins measured in the blood and the creatinine levels. It's just a matter of time. I'm in bed till 1 p.m. tomorrow because of the biopsy. They are hopeful for the kidney, so it's just a matter of time. Dialysis tomorrow!

Friday, 5 February 1982

Well, today I went on dialysis for 5.5 hours to get the potassium level down because it had gone up overnight, probably due to the biopsy. The funny thing was that by the time I went on dialysis, the level had gone down again. So for the first time, I've been on dialysis for no real reason except for a bit of a blood clean-out. Dr Rudder wanted me on for the full 5.5 hours. I don't know why. I'll ask him tomorrow, if I see him. It just seems funny being dialysed to keep the potassium level stable when it is normal. All other dialysis that I have had has been to remove the potassium, so it was just a bit strange.

Tomorrow I find out about the biopsy!

Monday, 8 February 1982

I may have to go on dialysis again today, but we'll have to wait and see. Yesterday, I think I passed a bit more urine than normal, but whether it is real urine or not, that is the question. The reason for this is that you can pass urine, as such, but it may not contain the right amount of toxins to be removed from the body. It is good to lose fluid that way, but it may also mean that the kidney is not filtering the blood properly, so I would still need dialysis. There are so many questions that I don't know the answers to. I'd like to wait and talk to the doctors about my fluid intake and the output, as I am still only on 800 mls/day.

It's late at night now and the ward is pretty quiet. I phoned Mum tonight and spoke to her. I must admit it was pretty good talking to her for a while about things, as it does get very lonely in here. I was able to give her some good news that the kidney still has a good chance of working, according to the results from the biopsy. I need to relax and take things as they come. I think the kidney will work in the end, but it may just take time.

I don't think I'm producing a lot of urine but with the dialysis and the biopsy, etc. It will take a while for things to work themselves out. My urine today was very dark, but I think that's because of the disruption of the kidney by the biopsy. Anyway, if there is anything that I need to be worried about, the doctors will tell me. But I think

I have a good chance. I shouldn't blow it by getting anxious about dialysis, etc. I'm getting tired now so I'd better get some sleep.

***

[Looking back, I really missed my parents, especially Mum, during the transplants. She understood me a lot better than Dad, and it was a lot easier to talk to her about what was bothering me, mainly the isolation and loneliness. I always felt Dad wanted me to show that tough, stiff-upper-lip attitude and make the most of it. I wasn't always able to do that, especially during the transplants. I found out later that Dad was just as understanding as Mum but found it difficult to show how much he cared.]

***

Tuesday, 9 February 1982

I really had a good night's sleep last night. So I think I'll stick with those half-dose pills that the psychologist put me on. I feel more relaxed and a lot more awake.

One of the new patients seems to be going really well. Her kidney is working, which is great. She looked really well yesterday. I think she is going to be busy with the doctors today. She seems to be doing the best out of all of us in the front room. Who knows? Anyone's kidney could start working at any time. It just seems to be a waiting game. Waiting and patience are what is needed in this type of situation. I'm glad that I'm in good hands.

I spoke to Mum and Lin earlier tonight and talked for a while. I've also still got the left drain in. It seems that the surgeons want to wait until the drain output is minimal before they take it out.

Wednesday, 10 February 1982

New day. I seem to pass more urine, but I still need to go on dialysis tomorrow, if the kidney doesn't work overnight. One positive thing to look forward to is that I will have an orange. I can't have them at the moment off dialysis because the kidney is not working. Oranges contain a heap of potassium, which is no good if you don't have a working kidney. I must admit it would be great to wake up in the middle of the night and produce a stack of urine. I'd be the happiest man in this ward. The drain is still draining, but not sure if it is slowing down or not. I am feeling tired tonight so I think I will sleep well.

Thursday, 11 February 1982

Dialysis again today as the kidney didn't work last night. But like I said yesterday, at least I can have an orange on dialysis. It's late Thursday night and I am waiting to go to bed after dialysis, but the sisters need to change the dressing on my drain because it was leaking. One of the nurses says peroxide will clean it up without hurting. I'm just going to relax and let them change the dressing so I can get some sleep.

Late Friday, 12 February 1982

I had four hours of dialysis again today. My levels were still very high from dialysis yesterday, so they had to dialyse me again and ...

Saturday, 13 February 1982

I was so tired yesterday that I couldn't finish the entry. I feel much better today. I saw Mum and Dad for about an hour. It was really great to see them, talk to them, and see how they look. I don't see many people as we can't normally see them in isolation. I really missed them over these past weeks in here, even Dad, the eternal worrier. Maybe that's where I get it from. I still missed him and it was great to see him. Dad looks thinner as a matter of fact, but he looks good and so does Mum.

I feel really good today, even though my potassium is a bit high. I'm trying not to worry about it. I just need to leave it to the doctors. To be honest, I really prefer not to know if my levels are high because I'll most probably just worry about them. I can't do anything about the levels other than do what the doctors say. I just hope that I don't need to take too much Resonium.

Resonium is a revolting drink that is like drinking chalk. Because I am on a low-fluid restriction, it normally is very thick, depending on how much I need to take, and it also makes me constipated. I don't mind taking a small amount to reduce the potassium, but I can't handle another big dose. The thought of it just puts me clean off! You never know, I may not even need any Resonium one day (cross fingers, thumbs, etc.).

Overall I feel pretty good today.

**

[Resonium is used to bring the potassium level in the body to an acceptable level, so that the patient does not have to dialyse as often. It contains sodium polystyrene sulfonate, which is known as an ion-exchange resin. It acts in the gut to exchange the sodium for potassium, thereby reducing the potassium level. These days doctors more often seem to give patients sodium bicarbonate capsules instead.]

**

Sunday, 14 February 1982

Well, at long last I got my final drain out today. Boy, it feels funny. I got used to it because it had been in for such a long time. It feels strange not having something hanging out of me any more.

Right now I'm sitting in bed, just relaxing a bit. I know it was only removing the drain, but I get a bit nervous about things like that. It's because when the drain is pulled out, I feel like it will pull out the kidney or part of the stomach, as it has been in for a long time and there is a lot of suction. The drain was about 20 cms long, so it looked like a snake. Anyway, maybe now you can understand why I was a bit nervous. I guess I need time to get myself together and then I'm okay. I never like these things being pulled out from me, especially that long. I don't mind cannulae or needles, but things like drains and catheters I don't like staying in for a long time. I guess it feels like, subconsciously, it's going to grow onto something, even though I know it won't. I'm just glad to get the drain out!

The day has gone without too much excitement. My temp is okay. I'll be having dialysis for six hours tomorrow, so that will make me feel better most probably. Right now I can't wait to have a shower, which I hope will be tomorrow morning. I haven't had a proper shower because of the drain. Again, it's great to get that drain out …

Monday, 15 February 1982

New day! Everything went wrong!

Dialysis was terrible. The machine kept breaking down and I got a really high temp, which I think has gone now because I feel quite cool. I'm having a cup of tea and going to bed to sleep away my worries, which I think is what I need.

Good night!

Saturday, 20 February 1982

Yesterday, I had another biopsy and they took two samples. I didn't get much of a sleep last night because of where the sandbag was. It was on my ribs and hurt a bit, so the ribs were uncomfortable, but they feel better this morning. They put me back on Amphogel (used to reduce phosphate levels in the blood) again because of my phosphate level. That's the way it goes. I was also put on a gram of Prednisolone (an anti-rejection drug) yesterday. I'll be on half a gram today and a quarter gram tomorrow. I don't know if I'll see anyone this weekend, but I hope so.

The new patient, with a transplant from her sister, is going home today, so that is great.

I just hope I don't have to go on a dialysis machine this weekend. I've had enough of it for a while. Everything seems to have happened to me this week on it.

- Monday – dialysis pump broke down.
- Thursday – spent 6.5 hours on it instead of 6. Somebody forgot to change the chemical over which checks the clotting time of the blood, so I spent an extra half an hour on the machine. In addition to that, I had a high temp of 39 deg. C, which didn't make me feel better. I just hope I can last the weekend, fingers crossed.

Funny thing happened today. My haemoglobin was 5 this morning and they needed to get some pack cells ready for a blood transfusion. But when they got the results for the test that they took later today, my haemoglobin was 6. They either made a mistake or my kidney may be on the way to working. Let's hope and pray that they didn't make a mistake, but there's always a human element. I remember from one of my first economic essays, that the human element is 'always a variable', and when it comes to blood tests, there is always a possibility that they got it wrong.

Here's hoping my little baby (kidney) has started to wake up, cross fingers.

Wednesday, 24 February 1982

Well, nothing much happened on Sunday, Monday, or Tuesday except for an occasional high temp and drip or drop of urine, and also a scan and ultrasound yesterday.

One good thing was that the scan from yesterday was better than the previous, and also the ultrasound looks good (i.e., no collection around the kidney). Yesterday I started on ALG again (another anti-rejection drug) which is a six-hour drip. I don't know how many I will be given. I think they give you three in a complete treatment and then swap you back to steroids, so you get a variation of the treatments and not just the steroids.

One great thing happened today. I passed 120 ml of urine in one go. I can tell you, that is an achievement and record, apart from the fact that I had diarrhoea as well. Anyway, I'm going to bed. Goodnight!

Thursday, 25 February 1982

Today I had dialysis again for six hours, and for the first time everything went right with it for the whole six hours. It looks like my temperature is due to something else, which I knew, but what else could it be? The only other times I had the temp was when I was on dialysis. Anyway, it's back to square one again. I don't know if the dialysis machine is doing the job of the kidney or the kidney is working until the doctors say something. But I think the kidney is starting to work because the urine I'm passing is darker. Also I have been passing a lot more than previously. Only time will tell.

Dr Rudder will tell me if I can get a weekend pass tomorrow. I hope so, but I've got a bit of a cold so he may not. I don't know what's best. I want to go home.

Tuesday, 2 March 1982

I went home for a day on Sunday. It was really great to get out! Mum picked me up and we went to see how my parents' house at Windsor was going. It is being built from new. We also saw Luke, Pearse, Adam, and Glenn on the way through, at their place. We just stopped off briefly. They were keen to find out how things were going, but I couldn't really tell them much. I found out that

Pearse and Luke are still playing at the Hero of Waterloo, Hotel in The Rocks, Sydney, and I must admit I did miss playing my guitar.

When we got home to the house my parents rent in Telopea, Mum cooked a lamb roast. It was delicious! One thing that I picked up while I was with them is that Mum and Dad are very worried about how the transplant is going, especially Dad. Which is understandable, as they are not used to the idea of kidney transplantation. It is so foreign for both of them. I must admit it was still good to get out of the hospital. I would like to get out more often, although hopefully I won't be in much longer.

According to Dr Chess, the latest scan, done today, has improved on the previous one. The kidney still looks good, and it's got a damn good chance of working. It's just taking a long time about it, but that's the way things go in a situation like this. I guess you just have to be patient and wait. With luck the transplant will be over quickly, and you have a successful kidney. If the transplant doesn't work, it's a fact of life. The machine is going to keep you alive until the next one comes along. Hopefully this transplant of mine is going to work and last for many, many a year.

I don't know what's being planned for me tomorrow. I may have the ALG drip again, but I don't know as they didn't say anything about it today. I'm a bit tired tonight after dialysis last night and the ALG drip yesterday, so I should sleep well. Except for my cold, I'm feeling pretty good. I'm going to improve, I'm sure.

Wednesday, 3 March 1982

The scan that was done yesterday was good. It registered at 103, which is a pretty normal perfusion rate. The question is why isn't the kidney working like a kidney with that perfusion. I'll have to ask Dr Rudder about it, but I can't do much about it really. I can just hope that things are on my side and the kidney will start to work and last forever. Until further notice, it's dialysis as usual tomorrow.

Saturday, 6 March 1982

Well, today hasn't been one of much production. As far as I know, the kidney is still sleeping and looks like remaining so for quite a while. I don't know what I can do to get things going. I guess I just have to sit back and wait, which is the most frustrating part about it.

Last week they put up my fluid restriction to 1500 ml, but I don't know if that was such a good idea. After dialysis last night (when I lost 4 kg) I haven't produced much urine at all, only 17 ml, which isn't much. I'm hoping that's just because of being a bit dry. I can only wait and see what happens in the morning.

Tomorrow I should be going home for the day, so that should be fun. I'm a bit worried about my weight. When I came off the machine last night, I was 56 kg. I think I've put on a bit of fluid, and I don't know what's wrong. Tonight I'm 57.5 kg, so I've put on 1.5 kg during the day. I hope I can pass a bit more urine in the morning, at least 80 ml. Other than that I should have a good day out tomorrow (Sunday) with Mum, Dad, Luke, and Pearse.

Wednesday, 10 March 1982

Well, it's been a while since I wrote in the diary, so I thought that before I went down to theatres, I'd write something.

Sunday was really great. I had the day out as planned and saw all the family again. The Windsor house is coming along really well. Monday I had dialysis. It was going really well until I came off and found out I had a temp of 38.9 deg C. That spoiled the rest of the evening for me.

Tuesday I went for a scan. Apparently it was as good as the previous one, so that was good news. The only problem is that I have now found out that I'm going down to theatres today for a look in my bladder and tubes, to see if there is any blockage in the system. The kidney should be producing a lot more urine, but it's only producing a small amount. So they are going to knock me out and take a look. Apparently it doesn't take long, but I have been on 'nil by mouth' since midnight. No breakfast for me today.

Two good things can come out of this. They may find out what has been causing the spike in temperature I sometimes get. Also I may be able to pass more urine if they can find something that needs to be corrected.

Thursday, 11 March 1982

The result of the inspection was that all was clear. That's good news in one way but bad in another, because now there's nothing to correct. I will have to wait and see when the kidney will work, and when that is, who knows.

I'm going home Sunday for a day again, so that will be good. Also I'm having another biopsy tomorrow, which I'm not really looking forward to but I guess it has to be done. I am sure you can understand I am a bit worried about having dialysis after it, because I will likely bleed. Anyway, they know what they are doing. I guess I'm just nervous! Other than that I feel quite good, in fact *great*.

Sunday, 14 March 1982

Today is my last day in the transplant ward. I'm going home for a day and then going to a different ward. A new transplant patient is coming in, and they need the bed. As I've been here the longest and theoretically am the fittest, I'm being moved out. I'm really glad to get out of here. I just hope I've got a bed to go to!

[I ended up moving to a new ward called A6.]

Wednesday, 17 March 1982

Today is going to be a big day. I'll most probably find out if they are going to leave the kidney in or take it out. The reason for this is the latest scan. It appears that it wasn't as good as the previous one, and my creatinine went up from 200 to 500, which is a bit of a jump. The doctors want to see if there's still good blood flow to the kidney. With some luck, the arteriogram will show that there is still blood getting to the kidney. If that turns out to be true, they will leave the kidney in and I'll still have a chance of a successful transplant.

I hope the kidney is still okay, because I don't really want to go back on dialysis. I guess I shouldn't give up hope yet. One good thing in my favour is that my previous scans have improved before. I just hope there is still blood getting to my kidney.

Here's to hope and faith. I must keep *both*!

***

That was the last entry in this diary. I ended up passing out on my bed with a temperature of about 48 degrees Celsius. It turned out that the spikes in temperature that I had been suffering were due to viral listeria meningitis.

I assume on the same day, 17 March 1982, I was taken to the operating theatre to have the kidney removed, as that was the only way I could survive. They could not combat the meningitis while I was on the immunosuppression for the kidney transplant.

I was put in the intensive care unit (ICU) for a several days in a coma. Apparently I had extremely high temperatures and suffered from fits. They thought I was going to die. The nurses told me that one of the doctors tried to stop me from having a fit, and I gave him a left hook which sent him flying. The nurses didn't like that doctor much, but I got on with him really well, so I'm not sure how true that was. He was about four times my size – a big lad.

During my time in ICU, the only things I remembered were floating towards a bright light for ages and my memories just passing me by. It was like being in an aquarium, walking through a tunnel under the water, except there weren't sharks on the other side of the glass. There were faces of people that I had known.

One of the last things I remember before I woke up was hearing my doctor talking. Someone said – or maybe I just had a feeling – that it wasn't my time to die. I then had a sensation of drifting back, away from the light and into consciousness. I'm not really sure why I experienced what I did. I do know that it was very peaceful and something I will never forget.

I woke up on my twenty-first birthday (22 March 1982) still on dialysis. The nurses had a cake for me. It was good to be alive and see them again – but I still didn't have a working kidney!

I was discharged from the hospital on 2 April 1982, after approximately two and half months in hospital. After another several months to recover, I went back to work. I was very lucky to have a job in the public service during that period of my life.

I think during this transplant I started to realise that life was too short. I needed to make the most of my life with no regrets. You don't have a lot of control over what happens in your life. Don't get me wrong – I have made mistakes in my life. But most of these came about from me trying to take control.

I also started to realise that no matter how much I wanted to achieve my goals, the how and when of achievement was mostly out of my control. All I could really do was relax and go with the flow.

6

The Third: Short and Sweet – Pneumonia

The next year, 1983, started off with me not knowing what I was going to do or where I was going live. I was having trouble living at home in Windsor, but I didn't have other options.

At work, I was able to transfer to the Department of Social Security, Windsor branch, on 16 May 1983. I did all right while I was there. I was promoted from the entry level grade, Clerk Class 1, to Clerk Class 2/3, and in those days that was an achievement.

I continued to work with my brothers and stayed with them most weekends. This certainly helped me handle living with my parents. I got to know a few other musicians, whom I started working with. One of them helped me find my own style as a soloist. I was still very much in my brothers' shadow when it came to music.

I had a great conversation one night at the All Nations Club, talking another musician about working with brothers. After that discussion, I decided to be myself and follow what I really wanted in music. That turned out to be quite a broad selection of music, from blues through jazz to soul. I think I made a good decision, but I know I would never have even attempted becoming a musician without the support of my brothers.

A lot of things were happening in my life, and I was beginning to find my way for a change. Then things went up in the air again when the next transplant was offered to me. I didn't expect it to happen so soon after the previous attempt. I went back to the hospital on 4 August 1983.

I didn't keep a diary for this transplant. It followed the same format as the previous two. This was the first time I spent in the new transplant ward, and my stay didn't seem as long as the previous transplants. Again the transplant was a sleeper – I didn't pass urine, and I went through a similar process of tests, tests, and more tests to find out why the kidney wasn't working.

Even though I wasn't very well, I dealt with the transplant in a positive way, but again it wasn't working. It turned out that I was developing pneumonia. The doctors didn't realise this was happening until they gave me a pass out of hospital one night. I started coughing straight away and couldn't breathe properly. That evening I tried to sleep, but my breathing got worse and my family had to rush me to hospital.

I wasn't in a good way.

Next day, I ended up having the transplant removed. I woke up on dialysis again. They were in the process of inserting needles into an artery in my wrist to check blood gases. I wasn't getting enough oxygen, so I also had an oxygen mask on.

I was discharged from hospital on 17 September 1983. It took a month or two to get over that transplant, but I eventually did and went back to the old routine of dialysis and work.

Soon after I had recovered, I decided that I needed to move out of my parents' house. My relationship with them was becoming very strained. My renal consultant told me how a hospital in Canberra had established what they called a satellite dialysis unit. I asked him to find out if there were any places available and whether he would mind if I transferred. He was very happy for me to do this; he knew what I was going through at home.

I applied for a job transfer to Canberra as well and was successful. So at the age of 23, in 1984, I moved to Canberra. For the first time, I could dialyse outside the hospital without having a machine in my home or living with my parents.

The move to Canberra was very important to me. It gave me the lifestyle I had longed for. I was able to continue working, and I was able to continue with music on my own terms.

I did very well in the social security department in Canberra. I transferred in as an administrative service officer (ASO) 2/3, was made an ASO 4 within twelve months, and then became team leader in 1986.

As team leader, I was given the task of training the Australian Capital Territory Regional Officers in a new computer system. I soon realised I had a knack with computer software. I decided that I wanted to move into computing, which I did a few years later in the social security central office.

The most recent failed transplant gave me a view on my future, to a degree. My body was only able to function effectively if I looked after it. It has been hard throughout my life for me to keep a focus on a healthy lifestyle. In those early years on dialysis, I didn't have a great view of my longevity, so I pushed my body quite hard.

Now, I am very thankful for each and every day that I am alive. It has always been a matter of getting a balance, having a good time, and looking after myself. I had nearly died for a second time during this transplant. I didn't want to regret doing something, but I also didn't want to regret *not* doing something when the opportunity arose.

My friends would have said that I tended to take any opportunity that I could, when it came to performing music or doing my job.

Most nights when I wasn't on dialysis, I was out playing or watching friends play. It was rare that I spent a quiet night at home.

But most nights weren't late. I never drank much because of the fluid restriction. In a way, the discipline of dialysis helped ensure that I was always able to perform my duties in my day job. I still had a good time.

Achieving a balanced lifestyle is an individual's choice. The healthier you are, the better your body can cope with any major medical condition. You just need to take time to work out your lifestyle balance and enjoy life. Moving out of my parents' home to Canberra was the best way for me to start finding balance for myself, and I had fun along the way.

7

The Fourth: Femoral Nerve Severed

I received a phone call on 28 August 1986 from the hospital in Sydney. I couldn't believe that I was being given another opportunity for a life free of dialysis. They had found a fourth perfect match. I was 25 years old.

And for the fourth time, I ended up with sleeping kidney. This went on for about a month, with all the usual tests and et cetera. I didn't keep a diary during this transplant, but as compared to the others, I spent a short time in hospital. The transplant itself was straightforward and I felt fine. I just was not producing urine. My blood levels were only kept in the normal range by dialysis.

As I had been through this so often, I knew a lot of the transplant staff, and we were quite close. With the odds of success falling as each day passed, the doctors needed to make a decision. They gave me two options.

- Leave the kidney in and remain on the transplant drugs, with a remote possibility that the drugs would reverse the current rejection.
- Take the kidney out before it started causing me problems.

In hindsight, I probably should have told them to leave it in, but I made the decision to have it taken out. That was an error in judgement on my part – but I still consider that I made the right decision.

Everybody wants to live what they perceive to be normal lives. When I made the decision to take out the kidney, I thought I would go back to what had become normal for me. That is why I believe that I made the best decision for me at that time.

Now, when things don't turn out the way you want, you may feel cheated. But you have to accept that the decision was still the *right* decision for you at the time that you made it.

Before I went into the surgery to remove the kidney, I had been feeling well and excited about moving forward with my life on dialysis. I had decided this transplant was going to be my last. I wanted to get better, go back to my life outside the hospital, and potentially take some time out or go on holiday.

When I woke in the recovery unit, I complained to the nurse that my right leg was numb. She gave me a strange look and said, 'Are you sure?' She said that she needed to get the surgeon to talk to me. I didn't understand what was going on.

The surgeon came over and explained what had happened while I was in surgery. Basically, there was a lot of scar tissue around the transplanted kidney. The femoral nerve to my left leg had been caught up in the scar tissue, and it was cut by mistake when they tried to remove the kidney. I had no idea what this meant at first; then, when he finished explaining, I realised what had happened and couldn't believe it. 'What else can go wrong, and why me?'

The femoral nerve controls the muscles to the knee. Without it working, at least to some degree, it isn't possible to walk unaided. Without control of the muscles, the knee cannot support you and keep you stable so you can walk.

When the surgeons realised what had happened, they needed to work out what to do, and quickly. They decided that the best way to fix it was to sew the nerve back together via microsurgery. For that, they needed to get hold of a specialist – a microsurgeon.

I do not know how long it was before they found one, but I am glad they did. It seems a microsurgeon was operating in the next theatre. They wheeled me from my theatre to his for an emergency nerve reconstruction. I don't know what the exact timing was, but I was very lucky.

The view of the medical staff was that the chances of me walking again were not very good. None of them had experienced this complication before. They weren't very sure of the prognosis.

All I could do was cope with it. I was always well looked after, but at that point I was not in a great state of mind. All I could think about was taking the surgeon to court for negligence. When it came to discussing my leg with any of the medical staff, I felt like I had the plague. But I still needed to work with the doctors who were looking after me. While I was healing, the surgeon who had done the operation was very supportive and made sure I had everything in place before I went back to Canberra.

I saw physiotherapists every second day. The hospital's occupational health technicians developed a sling so that I could use crutches as well as a wheelchair. The nerve had been severed in my left hip, and they wanted me to make sure I did not straighten my leg. They wanted me to always keep my left femur at 90 degrees to my hip so that the nerve would not be torn again by stretching.

Before I went home to Canberra, I also had to see the microsurgeon. The meeting was brief. He made sure I was able to get around on the crutches. He also referred me to a neurosurgeon in Canberra who would help with the nerve regeneration.

They gave me a wheelchair and a sling for my leg, to use when I was on crutches, when they discharged me from the hospital. The sling was not meant for continuous use; I didn't have control of my leg in the sling, and it could have damaged any recovery. I only used it when I was at home.

When I got back to Canberra, I mainly used the wheelchair. The nerve took a long time to regenerate. I wasn't sure if it ever would. My leg was strapped up so as not to disrupt the regeneration of the nerve, and I had to sleep with my hip at 90 degrees for about eight months.

That time in the wheelchair was mentally difficult. I really needed to stay positive, but I wasn't able to do it all the time. I got pretty depressed. Also, I was still on dialysis. I kept on asking the same questions: What did my future hold now? How would I get over this?

I wanted to take the surgeon to court for what he had done to me, but when I tried, I couldn't prove any negligence. My solicitor wasn't able to find another transplant surgeon to support a case of negligence, and we didn't have the money to pay for additional solicitors to take the matter further.

Obviously, music was still very important in my life. It kept me focused on other good things rather then what I was dealing with at that time. The blues had become my best friend.

One night that stands out in my memory was when my mates from a local bar called Kimbo's picked me up and took me and my wheelchair to the bar for a drink. I had played at Kimbo's before the transplant happened, so they knew me pretty well. Instead of wheeling me in at the back of the bar, they wheeled me into the front, near the stage. The bar was packed with all my friends.

What they did then still brings a tear to my eye. They took the wheelchair arms off, handed me a guitar, placed a mike in front of me, and said, 'Phil, sing us a song.' I was so emotional that I could hardly speak. I sang them a couple of my favourite blues tunes, 'Stormy Monday' and 'Need Your Love So Bad'. That night,

I realised what friendships were all about. Without my family, friends, and music, I think my life would have been the worst experience I could ever think of.

That night at Kimbo's was magical. I will never forget it or my friends who organised it for me.

While I was confined to a wheelchair, I stayed with my brother Josh. I was under regular physio and saw the microsurgeon in Canberra every few months. It took a considerable length of time to straighten my leg. I continued therapy until I was able to use a caliper for my left leg. The Canberra Hospital technicians built the caliper so that the knee joint locked, replacing the lost muscle control and enabling me to walk.

One of the challenges I had was to stimulate the femoral nerve. My objective was to walk again without any callipers. But the muscle had wasted in my left leg, so I had to build it up. I saw a nerve specialist in Canberra regularly for sessions to stimulate the nerve growth. This lasted about twelve months, as they felt that this was the length of time it would take to stimulate as much of the nerve regeneration as was possible.

The way they stimulated the nerve was to insert very thin needles into my leg. They were similar to acupuncture needles and about six inches long. Each needle had an electric charge connected to it so that the nerve impulses would be stimulated.

Eventually, the nerve re-grew to a point that I could move from the caliper that had a locked knee joint to one that was flexible. I was going to prove the surgeons wrong. It took nearly two years, but I moved from wheelchair to calipers to walking stick, and then I was free again.

I had made the decision to take myself off the transplant list. I had had enough. My body had been through enough pain. Instead of more surgery, I planned a holiday.

The doctors and nurses did not support this decision. Not many people went on holidays while on dialysis in those days. I had to plan it myself. They did give me some contacts to write to in South Africa and the UK, which was very helpful. Otherwise the trip would have taken me even longer to organise.

I planned a six-month holiday across South Africa and the UK, went, and had a ball. It had to wait several months to get confirmation for dialysis at different centres. Then, after getting rid of the caliper and strengthening my left leg, I flew out from Sydney on 1 December 1988 for the holiday of a lifetime, still on dialysis.

I think my determination to plan and take this trip helped me later in life when things got on top of me. I felt a successful transplant was out of my reach. I was single-minded about what I wanted after I was confined to the wheelchair, and my friends and family helped me through.

This determination has helped me in many ways, but it has also meant that I have tended to be a loner. I have found it easier to handle problems on my own, so they didn't impact anyone else. I guess it's because of that stiff-upper-lip philosophy that I learnt from my dad.

8

Trip of My Lifetime: First Stop South Africa

I had the best send-off I could ever ask for from the Kimbo's crew. It was one of those nights that you just didn't want to end: all my friends were there, the music was great, and the drinks kept flowing. Sticking to Scotch on the rocks to kept my fluid intake to a reasonable level. We had a fantastic night.

I flew out from Sydney 1 December 1988. I couldn't believe I had spent pretty well a year saving, planning, and writing letters to overseas consultants so that I could have my holiday. Finally, I was on my way, with my guitar in hand! First stop, Johannesburg and the rest of South Africa for three months, then travelling the UK for three months.

When I got on the plane, it was like a huge weight had been lifted off my shoulders. It hadn't been easy to plan the trip, and part of me had believed to the end that I wouldn't be able to do it. Now I was on the plane, on my way to South Africa.

I stayed with my aunt Shirl and my grandmother while I was in Johannesburg, and dialysed at a nearby hospital. Aunt Shirl's place was a semi-detached house located in a nice area of Johannesburg called Melville. The hospital was a ten-minute drive away, so it worked out really well. My uncle Pieter lent me an old car so that I could drive to and from the hospital. I also drove it around Johannesburg, once I got the hang of driving in South Africa.

The nurses at the hospital were great, but the patients certainly didn't like to talk much. The dialysis machines were modern; I didn't have any issues while I dialysed in Johannesburg. A thing that blew me away was that one of the patients used to smoke on dialysis. Apart from the safety aspect, it smelt terrible. I didn't know how the nurses could allow it. Maybe it was because he had lost his legs. He was also pretty aggressive. I am sure it would not be allowed today. I know how hard it is to stop smoking, as I was a smoker for about fifteen years, but I should never have started and I am really pleased that I was able to stop.

Most of the people that I met in South Africa, both black and white, were very friendly, good people. The only occasion that I came across any aggression was when some guy didn't like the fact that I believed Nelson Mandela would be leading the country in a few years. My cousins had to step in before he took a swipe at me. I was soon proven correct. I know there are still issues in South Africa, but I believe that having Nelson as a leader was a good move. I hope South Africa can still achieve what I believe is its destiny: to help Africa as a whole to come together, and to become a leading nation in Africa and the world. I wonder if that guy ever changed his feelings about Nelson Mandela.

It felt like I had two hundred cousins in South Africa, including first, second, and third cousins. That made the time go very fast, as they all wanted to meet me, and I had a ball. One of my first cousins, Sharon, was my travel buddy. She is fantastic, and we had a great time. She and I are still very close to this day. My other first cousins were great as well. We always had a good laugh together.

My first trip with Sharon was to a place called Gold Reef City Amusement Park, which focused on the history of Johannesburg and gold mining. The displays included tribal dancing and the Gumboot Dance, which was performed by the miners in their gumboots, or Wellington boots. It was a traditional dance among the miners. How times had changed.

In Johannesburg, my cousins introduced me to Nando's chicken. I couldn't believe how good chicken could taste. Nando's was a chain of takeaway restaurants that I believe started in South Africa, but are now in several countries in the world, including the UK. Their Peri Peri sauce is delicious!

We certainly had some great nights out together. One in particular was a free dance party. The music sounded like it came from an Ibiza disco, which wasn't really my type of music. Afterwards, we went to a fun park and had a go on the rides, including a roller coaster and a thing called the Gravitron. I have never felt as sick as I did on the Gravitron.

I went to a cousin's place for New Year's Eve. We all got plastered, so we ended up staying there, as I was in no condition to drive home.

My uncle Pieter used to take us out to his allotment, which was like a small farm that he had outside Johannesburg to grow fresh vegetables and fruit. We picked peaches and whatever else he wanted. They were great days.

Aunt Shirl and I also went on a few short trips on weekends, between dialysis, including trips to the Valley of 100 Hills, Blyder River Canyon, Sun City Casino (located two hours from Johannesburg), my uncle George's farm, Durban, and my godfather Hugh's sugar cane farm, which was near the Kruger National Park, one of Africa's largest game reserves.

On a trip to Uncle George's farm, I borrowed his car (which had trouble starting) to drive to my godfather's sugar cane farm on my own. Hugh took me to the Kruger National Park, which was quite near to his farm. We ate a Sunday morning breakfast and saw some amazing animals, even though we were only there a short time – mainly elephants and rhinos. Hugh wanted me to come back for a full weekend later in my stay. It probably sounds crazy that we went for breakfast to a game reserve, but what else do you do if you are close enough to do it?

On the Monday morning, I drove back to Johannesburg after my godfather helped me push-start the car. I drove most of the way without stopping as I wasn't sure the car would start again. I did have to stop once for petrol. Luckily there was an attendant, and I asked him to fill the car while it was still running. He wasn't too keen about it, but he did it in the end. I gave him a big tip. That was one of the things that I liked about South Africa – the majority of people were very helpful.

I went to Durban by bus, and the air conditioning wasn't working. It reminded me of those movies about going on a safari in the heat of Africa, but in this case I was on a proper bus and not a big four-wheel drive. I stayed with another aunt in Durban for two weeks and caught up with more cousins, who showed me around Durban when I was off dialysis.

I borrowed an Alpha Romeo from one of my cousins to drive while in Durban. It was a huge bonus in terms of seeing the sights and travelling to dialysis. On one trip in the Alpha, my cousin Judy and her husband Gerry took me to Kloof, which was quite far out of Durban in 1988. I also went on a trip with another cousin, Margaret, to the Wild Coast, which is in eastern Cape Province.

The dialysis machines in Durban were very old, nothing like the ones in Johannesburg. They were made of a variety of parts from different machines, but they worked. They were based on the original washing machine types on which I had started dialysis nearly a decade before. The ward was very big compared to Johannesburg, with ten times the number of patients. I was very glad I could look after myself and put in my own needles. I don't think the nurses would have had much time for me.

My trip to South Africa would not have been as exciting and enjoyable as it was if I had been travelling by myself. I was very lucky to have such a great extended family. The day I got back to Johannesburg, I just crashed out and slept. The return bus trip from Durban had been a lot better; I was just tired.

I did go to the Kruger Park for a whole weekend, which was amazing. Hugh, his wife Erica, their daughter Gillian, Aunt Shirl, and I went off early on the Saturday morning and stayed overnight in the middle of the park, at a place called Satara, one of the enclosed camps.

We saw antelope, warthogs, elephants, kudu (a large antelope), giraffes, wildebeests, and zebra. We also saw a lion kill, which was amazing and sad at the same time. At Satara, we were treated to an evening serenade from the lions that were hunting outside the camp. The walls of the camp were about twenty feet high, so there was minimal chance of the lions getting over.

We made our way back to the farm on the Sunday via Blyde River Dam and Canyon, the Three Rondavels (mountain peaks), Bourke's Luck Potholes (name after Tom Bourke, an unsuccessful prospector), Mac Mac Falls (named after the Scottish miners who tried to find gold there in the 1879 gold rush), and of course God's Window viewpoint, where the cliffs drop an amazing seven hundred metres to the lowveld. Aunt Shirl and I headed back to Johannesburg on the Monday morning early, to get me back for dialysis in the afternoon.

On one trip from Johannesburg, we went to a casino called Sun City. We had a great time but lost all the money I had budgeted to lose. I have always taken a set amount to casinos and enjoyed the experience with only that amount. Whether I win or lose, I still have a good time.

The most memorable trip to my uncle's farm was when I met one of my second cousins, Kerry. We got on great. She showed me around the farm, including the old milking shed and the chicken coop where they were raising chicks.

When we went to the old milking shed, we noticed that a horse had got in there by mistake. She asked me to stop it from getting out of one of the entrances while she calmed it down. She then would take it out to the pastures. The problem was that I didn't realise there was mud and who knew what else at the entrance I was guarding. When I stepped there, my leg disappeared up to my knee in mud. I had flip-flops on, not proper farm boots, and lost one in the muck. I definitely was not going to reach in and try to find it.

Obviously, my cousin and everyone else on the farm killed themselves laughing when they found out what happened. I can't really blame them. It taught me that I should wear proper boots when I went walking on a farm!

The Old Milking Shed

In Johannesburg again, my cousin Stephen, whom I had tried to meet up with, eventually contacted me. I went over to his place for dinner to meet him and his wife. He was working as part of the trade unions to help promote equality in the workplace. He was quite an amazing guy. He invited me to see a play with him and his fellow workers. It was part of their training. I decided to go, and I was very pleased that I did, as we ended up seeing *Sarafina*.

Sarafina is about the Soweto riots, how a girl survived them and wanted to promote a better society. I found it very powerful. I realised then that South Africa wanted change. But the authorities at that time were not willing; they were scared. That is why I felt that they needed to get Nelson Mandela to help. South Africa still has problems these days, but the balance is getting better. I don't think that there is a simple solution even now.

As part of our night out, we went to a jazz club next to the theatre. What a night of music that was. We may have been the only white guys in the club, apart from the sax player onstage but I never felt more comfortable. It was like the political world outside didn't exist. That night will remain in my memories for a very long time.

My cousin Sharon, who had been my travel buddy over her summer holidays, had gone back to her last year in high school. I helped her with a biology experiment. She was assigned to show how a sheep's lungs changed as it breathed. Sharon had the camera, and I had the sheep lungs. It didn't turn out the best for me, but she got the photos she needed. It was my idea to blow up the lungs so that she could get a good picture, but when the sheep lung blew back, I got mouth full of disgusting sheep lung gases. I didn't find it funny at the time, but Sharon and the rest of the family found it hilarious. It is still one of the most stupid things I have ever done. But my cousin passed her assignment.

I spent quite a bit of time with my uncle Pieter, and he arranged a farewell dinner for me. He introduced me to ox tongue. I still get a sick feeling in my stomach when I think about it. I kept imagining that I could feel the oxen taste buds. Realistically, it tasted like salted silverside (a cut of beef from the hindquarter of cattle), so wasn't too bad. If they hadn't told me it was ox tongue, I probably would not have noticed.

My time in South Africa was coming to the end, and it had just flown. I had met some fantastic people I was very proud to consider family. I couldn't believe I had been able to do all the things I had done, but then again, I had been determined to have a great time. My relatives certainly helped me enjoy my trip. I was able to forget about the problems I had had with the previous transplant.

9

Trip of My Lifetime: Next Stop the United Kingdom

I arrived in London on 26 February 1989 and stayed in the Walkabout Club (Hotel Royal Eagle) for a few days before I booked into the Youth Hostel Association (YHA) accommodation at Carter Lane, near St Paul's. I had organised dialysis at St Bartholomew's Hospital, which was very close – basically on the other side of St Paul's.

I had a crazy budget in those days. I had allowed £5 for lunch *and* dinner. According to my diary, I I kept to that budget, but I don't think I could do so these days. I mentioned in my diary that I had a Big Mac meal for £2.20 at McDonald's. In 2016, a Big Mac meal was £4.29. That's inflation for you.

The hotel I stayed at was reasonable. I had my own bathroom with a toilet, so for a cheap hotel, it was good value. I just couldn't afford to stay there the whole time I planned to be in London. Breakfast was included and I made the most of that, which helped me keep to my budget.

The first weekend in London, I spent most of the time walking around town. I went to Hyde Park and took a few photos. Winter was just about over. The daffodils were coming out, which was great for me. The weather was quite sunny but still very chilly.

I came across a grey squirrel and it seemed very friendly, so I put my hand out. Big mistake. It tried to bite me but only got a small nip. I learnt my lesson that day about the local wildlife. Obviously he thought I had something to eat in my hand. I still have a photo of the culprit.

The Squirrel

The worst part about the weather in the UK is that winter is grey and cold, which is not like Canberra. Canberra is sunny in winter after about ten o'clock in the morning, when the fog lifts. The other thing that bothered me was the taste of the London water. It tasted terrible, but I got used to it after a while.

I had a good view from my window at the hotel. The sun came streaming in during the morning, when there was sun. Across the road were blocks of flats; in fact the whole street was full of such buildings.

I spent just a few days in the hotel, and then I needed to get myself settled in at the Carter Lane YHA. I was going to be dialysing at St Bart's nearby, and I really needed dialysis. The youth hostel had a lot of character. It had been the residence of the St Paul's choir, so the dormitories were well used, to say the least. Nowadays, it's been renovated so that it has lost a bit of the old charm.

I met a guy there who was a ship restorer. He was in the UK doing research for the Canadian government. He had taken a few days off from the research, so I gained a tourist buddy for a day or two. We went to Trafalgar Square, Camden Market, London Museum, and the Postal Museum.

I was amazed by the variety of buildings and the amount of building work being carried out in London. The history in London's streets, let alone all the museums and galleries, was mind-blowing for a 26-year-old who had not seen much of the world's treasures. I could have spent weeks looking around the city.

Dialysis went well. I found a laundrette quite close to the hostel. Everything was going to plan. My first week in London was packed with seeing new sights, including the Guildhall, Barbican Centre, Madame Tussauds, the Planetarium, and the British Royal Centre. A good thing about London was that you could see so many things just by going for a walk. Even when I aimed to see one tourist sight, I ended up seeing many thing. There is so much to see in London. I also had a chance to see my first West End play, *The Mouse Trap*. It was excellent.

My budget held out, but it wasn't much. I was living on about £10 per day. I'd become a regular at the breakfast joint around the corner from the YHA. They knew what I wanted when I walked in, and the girl behind the counter always had my tea ready. It was a bit of fun having somebody in this massive city taking notice of a foreign tourist. With all the travelling I had done, I was still enjoying meeting new people and seeing new things.

When things go well for a while, I expect something to go wrong. It happened. I bombed my arm badly in dialysis. The worst part was that I had arranged a trip to Paris for the following weekend. It was the first time that I would experience being in a place where I didn't speak the language. The nurses had agreed that I could leave my guitar at the hospital while I was away. All I could do was hope that my arm would heal well enough in time for my trip.

And I was! The trip to Paris went really well. I only had one slight problem when I got to the Metro: I got on a train going in the opposite direction from where I wanted to go. I got off a couple of stations along and tried to find my way to the return platform. I ended up going out the exit instead – classic comedy routine.

Finally I got to a station near my hotel. I was pleasantly surprised by the room. The shower was fantastic. At least I didn't have to wait till two o'clock to get a hot shower, as I had to do at the YHA.

After the shower, I headed out for a meal. I found a little Italian restaurant around the corner, which was very nice. I got a chance to practice my French, badly. After dinner I went for a walk.

This was when I discovered I was staying in the red light district.

It wasn't that bad. To be honest, the girls were very pleasant and reminded me of Kings Cross in Sydney. Things don't change much, no matter what country you are in. I didn't stay out long because I was exhausted. I headed back to the hotel – by myself.

I learnt something about myself during that trip: I can be quite stubborn. When it came to asking for or accepting help, I preferred to sort things out myself. In Paris, that meant a lot of stumbling along until I got so frustrated that I asked someone. I had to learn to get over that, especially in a foreign country.

My tour around Paris went well. The main reason I had come was to see the Louvre, but annoyingly, it was closed for remodelling.

It was scheduled to reopen 30 March 1989, and I was there on 26 March!. I should have asked the travel agent when I booked the trip.

I still enjoyed my time. The bus trip that I took around the city went well, apart from the fact that they only gave us twenty minutes to see the Eiffel Tower. It took me thirty minutes to get up the tower and down again. Needless to add, I took a leisurely stroll through the streets of Paris to get back to my hotel.

That night I crashed. I had planned to leave the hotel about nine thirty the next morning, but only woke up at nine twenty. I dashed. Shower, breakfast, train station, and I just made the train at 11.05 a.m.

When we got to Boulogne, we were told the Channel was too rough for the hovercraft that was meant to be the next leg of our journey. We had to make our way to Calais and catch a ferry from there.

It was good to reach English soil again at Dover. But I still had to get back to the hospital for dialysis. I made it at eight o'clock that evening, and was on a machine by eight thirty. I slept through the treatment and woke up about six o'clock next morning. I felt half dead. *What a trip.*

Bristol – Dad's Family

Bristol was where my dad was from, and most of his immediate family still lived there. I met my dad's sisters when I arrived, just before I went off to the Glen Hospital for dialysis. The hospital was pretty impressive. I had my own room and a private nurse to look after me, which was something I wasn't used to. It went well. We just needed to adjust some of the machine settings to remove the excess amount of fluid I was carrying.

I stayed with my half brother, Roderick, for the rest of the week. We got on really well. It was the first time that I had met any of Dad's family from his previous marriage. Roderick was about 40 years old then, and his lifestyle was very different from mine. He was a fascinating guy, and I am very glad that I had the opportunity to get to know him.

Roderick took me to visit Dad's brother, Bruce, in Dartmouth. Bruce was a real card, an interesting character. He certainly seemed to like solitude, but he had a lot of great friends. He was not very well, but he had a fantastic attitude towards life. Maybe some of that was passed on to me.

Dad used to tell us a story about Bruce. Bruce decided to go live in a monastery in Spain in the 1960s. He turned up expecting to meditate and contemplate his life. They neglected to tell him that they were building an extension that summer. Everyone who stayed there had to help them with the building. As you can imagine, this wasn't the peaceful atmosphere he had expected. But he did help them, and I'm sure he enjoyed it.

Nottingham and Sherwood Forest – Home of Robin the Hood

I had always been a fan of Robin Hood, so I couldn't visit England without at least seeing Nottingham Castle and Sherwood Forest.

I took a bus from Bristol to Nottingham and arrived at the YMCA about quarter past one. The accommodation was fine, a private room with a shared shower on the same floor. The best thing was that the YMCA was only £32 per week, including breakfast. I wonder what it costs nowadays?

My stay in Nottingham had its ups and downs. The hospital had forgotten that I was coming to dialyse, so I was put in isolation on an old-fashioned machine. It didn't deliver the Heparin properly or dialyse me very well. Overall, it wasn't as bad as my experience in Durban, but the dialysis on that first day was about the worst I have ever experienced. I decided to contact the next hospitals on my itinerary – Edinburgh Hospital, Scotland, and Rhyl Hospital,

Wales – to confirm with them, just in case they had forgotten as well.

I visited Nottingham Castle, which is a manor house now, and Sherwood Forest, which was fantastic. It was only a thousand acres, where once it had covered the whole of Nottinghamshire. It made me think of how men and women have changed over the centuries. I think most of the changes have been for the best, but some of the positive values may have been lost or reduced to only a few people today.

The Jerusalem Pub

The Nottingham Castle grounds included an old pub at the bottom of the cliff that the original castle was built on. It was called the Jerusalem Pub. They had a story about a model ship that was on display behind the bar. The story goes that if anyone ever tried to dust the ship, they would die within twenty-four hours – a curse, in short. So no one had dusted it in centuries.

When I spoke to Edinburgh Hospital to confirm I was coming, they said they weren't aware of my plans. I had to wait and call back in a day or two to see if I would be allowed to dialyse there.

I had three options if I couldn't dialyse in Edinburgh Hospital: stay in Nottingham; go on to Rhyl Hospital earlier, as they had confirmed their availability; or go back to London and dialyse at St Barts. None of these options were great. I would need to extend my stay somewhere in every case, and I didn't really want to do that. I had been very lucky that Nottingham Hospital agreed to take me after the initial problems there, and I didn't want to push my luck.

I had become closer to the guy upstairs since I had been travelling by myself. It was good to think about things. Talking things through with the guy upstairs helped me cope on my own.

With the Edinburgh uncertainty heavy on my mind, I went to see the movie *A Fish Called Wanda*. It was hilarious – just what I needed to forget about my worries.

The following day I contacted Edinburgh again, and they confirmed that they could fit me in. I was so happy. Everything was coming together. I organised my accommodation in Edinburgh and Rhyl. The accommodation in Edinburgh was at a B & B, while the accommodation in Rhyl was a converted manor house right next to the Rhyl Hospital.

Edinburgh, Scotland – Home of my Mother's Ancestors

My mother's family originated in Scotland. She had ancestors going back to the Hayhurst and Armstrong clans, so we certainly had some Scottish blood in our veins.

My trip to Edinburgh from Nottingham by bus was overnight, which saved me money on accommodation.

When I got to Edinburgh, I booked into the B & B and then contacted the hospital about dialysis. They said I needed to be there at 10.00 p.m., so it would be a late night for me. While I was on dialysis, I met their renal registrar. He asked me what I was doing over here in the UK, so I told him. He said he could provide me with a map for motoring, which was great.

I hired a red car (they go faster) for the weekend, and the trip was fantastic. The scenery was magnificent. I stayed on a loch for the night and woke up to a foggy morning. There was a view of a small sailboat on the shoreline. I watched the fog rise while I was having breakfast. It was excellent.

The roads through the Highlands are very narrow and windy. You need to watch out what is coming your way, as there are only small areas in the road where one can pass another car or truck. On one stretch, I was going through a small hamlet. To my surprise, I came across another car coming towards me, but there was no way to pass. Luckily I wasn't going fast. I slammed on my brakes and came to a sliding stop about six inches away from the oncoming car. I had been coming down an incline and there was gravel on the road – very dangerous! But I managed not to damage either car or driver.

When I got back to Edinburgh, I changed rooms at the B & B and got my own shower in the new room, so I was very comfortable. The rest of my stay was fantastic. I focused on the local scene. I visited Edinburgh Castle and was impressed with history behind the clans and the castle. I sampled the local Scotch whisky, as I had become accustomed to drinking it, neat or with a bit of ice, over my years on dialysis. I went to the famous establishments along the Royal Mile. Several of them allowed patrons to sample a dram or two. I was in my element, and it was very educational.

I climbed up Arthur's Seat, which is the peak in Holyrood Park that gives a great view of the castle and of Edinburgh itself. I also did a bit of exploring to find good live music venues.

Rhyl, Wales

I decided to visit Rhyl mainly because they had a dialysis unit well situated for seeing the sights of Snowdonia. I wasn't disappointed.

I arrived in Rhyl by bus and caught a taxi to the manor house B & B I had booked. The manor house was amazing and was in the process of being renovated. My accommodation was the old stables, which had been converted to individual units. The staff looked after me really well. I had a few good nights out with some of them.

I visited the slate mines in Snowdonia National Park and travelled around Snowdonia. I also rode a train to the top of Mount Snowden. What a view I had that day.

The mine openings were scattered with slate as if there had been an explosion. I felt I had just walked onto a *Dr Who* set, and they were waiting for the Daleks to turn up. Entering the mines themselves was like entering another world of darkness, lit only by a few lights on the walls of the caverns. I was amazed how they were so cold and damp. I am sure the mines have changed since I was there in 1988, but at the time it was an incredible experience.

I was getting near time for my return to Australia, now only three and a half weeks away. I admit that at this point I was looking forward to getting home.

London – Home Away from Home

After my short stay in Rhyl, I returned to the YHA in Carter Lane, London. I had gotten to know quite a few of the people who worked there. One night they invited me to join them in their basement accommodation, which was like travelling back to the 1960s. They had set it up as a bohemian cellar, and it was fantastic. They had access to a small outside quadrangle with a table and chairs. They invited me to have a few drinks and bring my guitar. I ended up playing a few songs for them in the quadrangle that evening. Unbeknown to me, there were people hanging out from the dormitory windows above me. After I finished playing, they cheered and applauded me. It was great.

I went for an overnight stay to Oxford with one of the girls that I met at the YHA. I came back the following day and made a plan to go to Stonehenge from Victoria Bus Station.

I have always found Stonehenge an amazing piece of history and mystery. Stonehenge is a ring of standing stones that are believed to be associated with several burial sites and also considered an important site by the Druids. I don't know a lot about Stonehenge, but I am still drawn to it.

I also saw Bath, which is a historic site with stunning architecture built by the Romans, who conquered England many centuries ago. Again, I am no expert on Bath, but I find it very interesting.

In a nutshell, that was my big holiday. I couldn't believe I had done it! I had travelled around South Africa and England while maintaining my dialysis. I had left Sydney on 1 December 1988, and I landed back on Australian soil 22 May 1989.

***

Upon my return, I was given the opportunity to transfer into the central office and join the IT division. It took me several years to develop my skills, but I eventually joined the test team and became a test coordinator.

I moved to part-time hours in 1991, as I was finding working and maintaining dialysis difficult. I was lucky that my supervisors agreed that I could work three days a week. I continued to play music, both solo and in bands, so life was reasonably balanced.

With my travels, I had demonstrated that I could do whatever I wanted to. I accomplished a massive task, and the reward was immeasurable. I proved many things to myself, and maybe to a few other people along the way. I could do anything I wanted to on dialysis, as long as I took the time to plan.

I discovered that my freedom was just as important as my family, friends, and music. I developed friendships with my relatives that I would never have been able to if I had not travelled. I still am close to them today.

I also found out that I was becoming more spiritual in my way of dealing with life. It has helped me balance my life, then and now. I don't know if I have got it right, but I think that as you go through life, you experience challenges and things change. Sometimes you need to take time out to focus on what you really want. My six-month trip helped me get my new focus. This balance continued for quite a while, but gradually I found it more difficult.

10

Fifth and Last

This chapter is based on a diary I kept about the event that has had the most impact on my life so far.

Thursday, 16 December 1993

My life has just been turned upside down. My sister, Lin, has offered me one of her kidneys. I can't believe that after all this time, I may have a chance to have a normal life once more. It's been fifteen years since I went on dialysis, and I have had four unsuccessful transplants which have put my body through hell and back. The chance to have another transplant which is the best match I could ever get is mind-blowing. I'm feeling scared and happy at the same time. I want to make sure that the transplant has every chance for success, so I'm going to the professor in Sydney to see what he says and get the ball rolling.

It's funny. About a month ago, I had given up all hope of getting a transplant from anyone, let alone Lin, and now it's on my doorstep. I have no idea what will happen when the transplant works. I am a bit scared by the thought of experiencing normality. I don't really know what a normal life is like. I've been stuck on a machine three times a week for six hours over the last fifteen years. I've got to make sure this one has the best chance. It *will* work, with a bit of help from the guy upstairs.

Monday, 27 December 1993

I went to see the professor on 22 December. He seems confident that as long as the next lot of blood tests are all right, the kidney will stand a very good chance of working. The next blood test is to combine my lymphocytes with Lin's to see what happens. If they attack each other, the transplant will be called off, as far as I am concerned. The blood test will take at least one week to come up with the result. By that time I will be on holiday in Lismore with Mum and Dad. Basically, I've got a 50/50 chance to get a positive result from that test, but at least I do have a chance.

Apart from this, I have been very busy over the last few weeks with my big band, Midnight Express. We've been working two gigs per week, and let me tell you, they've been late ones but great. We have just lost one of our backing vocalists. Now starts the job of finding a new one. We have tried out one girl so far, and she seems good, but we have got two other girls to try out on Wednesday. We will see what happens with them.

I'm really looking forward to my holiday. I'm having four weeks off, and each day is going to be great. I hope to catch up with a few friends, but we shall see what happens.

The weather at the moment has returned to winter for some reason. I can't believe the sudden change. We have snow in the hills outside Canberra, and it's bloody cold.

Thursday, 13 January 1994

Well, I got the news yesterday about the test, and it appears it's all full steam ahead.

I still can't believe that this is happening to me. I'm sure reality will set in when I'm in the operating theatre. Lin is confident that it will work, which make me feel good, but still at the back of my mind there is a bit of doubt, mainly because I already have had four perfectly matched kidneys and they never worked. I must admit this doubt is slowly disappearing because it is such a good match, and we went the extra level with the additional blood test. I guess I'm scared of putting my body through another transplant and also the fact that Lin is going to have a massive operation herself. I pray that this one will work. I get the feeling that I'll be around for a few years yet. On 2 February 1994 I will start my new life.

I keep wondering what my new life will be like. Will I do amazing things? Will I be successful? Will Lin be all right? All these questions and no answers, yet.

I have a feeling that Lin will be fine. I keep dreaming about what it will be like having to go to the toilet. I was saying to Mum that every other transplant has *not* been planned, and this one happens to have everything planned to the nth degree. This means that with all things considered, this transplant will work. Lin will be fine and I can get on with *my* life, whereever it takes me and whatever that holds.

Tuesday, 25 January 1994

Well, the day is getting closer. Only one week before I get admitted to RPAH for my *last* transplant. You know I still can't really believe it's happening. It seems unreal that within the next two weeks, I will probably have a brand-new *life*. Last night Josh took a few photos of me to show what I look like now. I'll get some more taken when I get out of hospital, as a sort of photographic record of my progress.

I had a dream last night. I can't remember everything about it, but it was to do with the transplant. It was as if it didn't work straight away, but I have a feeling it all worked out fine. I think the reality is hitting Lin. She is getting a bit nervous, and I must admit I don't blame her, because I am too.

I wish I could do more to make sure that the kidney works. I've tried to relax and get my body in good condition, but there is only so much I can do.

I guess I have two wishes about this transplant. These are: 1. that Lin recovers well, without any hitches, and (I am going to be a bit selfish) 2. I want the kidney to work really well and give me a great new life so I can do just what I want to and try to achieve my potential.

I do realise that I won't be able to do everything at once. But as soon as it all settles, I intend to do as much as I can. I guess having a kidney will change my life for the better, but I'm sure all my troubles won't be solved. My left leg is still very weak as the muscles are still wasted after all these years. Maybe I should have exercised more. At least I will have a kidney firing on all cylinders! You know what? I may actually end up getting bored at home on the days that I would normally attend dialysis. That's a funny concept, but I'm looking forward to that feeling.

I know this may sound strange for me to say, and maybe I am slightly strange. But I am still alive for some reason, and after I have this transplant, I am going to make the most of my life and do all I can to find out what the reason is. Most of all, after I have the transplant and I get out of hospital, I am going to have a great time at a huge party when I feel better.

Tuesday, 1 February 1994

Well, here I am in the transplant ward. It's the same room I had when the ward was first opened. It hasn't changed much, still has the real hospital smell about it. I went on dialysis this morning and finished at 4.30 p.m. During this time I was prodded and poked by the prof and his assistant. The prof's assistant wasn't that impressive, but I am sure that he know what he's doing. I do hope the prof does all the surgery. I've had enough of people not knowing what is going on. I am sure the prof will make sure everything is fine this time. It's funny to think that five months ago, I didn't ever contemplate another transplant. But here I am, once again going through the motions.

My blood pressure was a bit high tonight, but when they took it just now, it was reasonable (150/90). I'll see if I can get a TV. I hope to catch up with Luke and Lin when they get here tomorrow, 2 February 1994, the start of my new life.

Today I hit my funny bone on my left arm, and boy did it hurt. I am still in pain. I want to keep a record on my aches and pains just to know what I had before I got in here. My right side, just near my rib, feels funny. I think this is because of my previous transplants. My cough is still there. I must remember to breathe deeply after the operation.

I want so much for this transplant to work, and I'm sure it will!

The transplant registrar just came in. He seems like a good bloke. He was able to fill me in on a few details that I wasn't sure about. My friends rang and wished me luck, but the doctor came so I couldn't really talk.

I'm having a sleeping tablet tonight because I'm definitely going to need one. The sister looking after me tonight is called Lyn. She seems quite nice. I'll be taken down to the operating theatre at about 7.30 a.m. I've also got to have immunosuppression before I go into the theatre. Another doctor is about to put a cannula in my arm, so this will probably be the last note that I write until tomorrow.

Wednesday, 2 February 1994 (Transplant Day)

They gave me Imuran and cyclosporin (CSA) by drip. I have just had my pre-med and I'm feeling goooood. I said a prayer to the guy upstairs to help guide the prof's hand.

The Imuran made my arm ache. The CSA has made me feel quite warm, but it's better than feeling cold. Both night sisters were very nice, and I slept well with two amazipan.

Monday, 7 February 1994

Well, it's the Monday after, and I have had the transplant. One of the things that happened when I went down to theatres was that the prof said they may need to attach a bag outside my body to act as an external bladder, as they did not know whether my bladder would work after all this time. You can imagine how happy I was when I woke up with a catheter instead. They took out my catheter today.

I am passing urine regularly, but my creatinine has gone up a bit, so they have started me on steroids (prednisone) treatment. I am still thinking really positive about the kidney. Lin says I should ask for spiritual guidance to help. I know that I haven't been very spiritual over the years, but I have asked for help to keep a positive outlook.

***

Success!

When they had taken all the tubes out and I was able to walk, I went to the hospital news agency and got Lin a card. I wanted to give her something to say thanks, so I wrote a poem and put it in the card. I later made the poem into a song called 'The Gift'. I recorded a CD with songs that I had written while I was on dialysis.

Unfortunately, the original poem never made the CD, as I lost the lyrics. I wrote another song to include on the CD. I am hoping to record the original the way I intended, and to release it around the same time of this book.

The Gift (Original)

Walking these streets
Just to pass the time
These endless streets
The corners of my mind
Wondering why, where, or when
This dream will ever end

You gave me a life
Generous and true
To me it was all
To you, it was you
My life will be free, free as a bird
Because of you, I have learnt the word

I cannot repay, with money or kind,
The gift that you gave
For the rest of my life
All I can say to you with love
I will live my life as free as a dove
For you, my sister, I give thanks, with love

***

Monday, 14 February 1994

Today is an amazing day. I'm out of the hospital for the first time with a successful transplant. This meant *no* more dialysis, as I am producing normal amounts of urine. The main thing now is to keep a check on the blood results to make sure the kidney keeps functioning.

I'm staying at the nurses' home over the road from the hospital, but at least I'm out and things are looking good. The weather outside naturally is warmer and I feel a bit warm, but I think that may be the nurses' home or the weather.

Wednesday, 16 February 1994

Day 14 and things are good. Yesterday was my first clinic, and that was a bit nerve-racking, but it's just a matter of getting used to a new routine. I found out that my white blood cells were up yesterday, so I have to have blood cultures done. I think it's because of the scar in my leg, which is where they took a vein to extend the connection to my aorta, so I have great blood flow to the kidney. The leg scar is still weeping, and the clips are still half in for both scars. The doctors are going to check me out anyway today. Hopefully I will get an answer about the scar from the surgeons sometime today. Last night was the best night I've had so far. I was still getting up in the night, but I am feeling rested. I'm sure things are going to get better once the scar in my leg heals.

The clinic sister told me today that cyclosporin (CSA) raises the potassium level, so I'll have to be more careful with potassium while the CSA level is so high. I had the CSA level checked today, and it will be interesting to see the results. I was really tired last night after all the running around during the day (basically going from one doctor to another, getting tests done).

All I really want is to be back in Canberra with my friends. I never thought Canberra would be first on my list and not Sydney. I know the reason why; it's because all my close friends are now in Canberra. Just pick up the phone to speak to them costs a small fortune while I'm in Sydney.

My creatinine from yesterday's test was up a bit, but they not concerned. I wonder what the standard situation is when they are trying to find what a good creatinine for an individual is? I guess it is still early days and I shouldn't be in a rush to get back to Canberra, but I think I have to do a few other things rather than sitting and waiting at the nurses' quarters. If I am still here next week, I'll have to get out more and do a few things. I have to give my Canberra doctor a call now and fill him in on what is happening, or at least what I know.

My doctor in Canberra was quite casual about when I was coming back, so that's good. I don't want to put his nose out of joint. He agrees that I should only go back to Canberra once everything has settled.

I went to visit one of the nurses at the dialysis unit, and we are going for coffee next Wednesday, which will be good. It's funny how she is still here after all these years. She doesn't look a day older than when I first met her, when she first dialysed me on peritoneal dialysis back in 1978. Sixteen years ago – I wonder what she has been up to? Most of the sisters who were around then are married, with kids, and settled. I was actually wondering what happened to the dietician as she was very attractive. She's probably married some doctor or lecturer. We got on really well, which shows what sort of person she was, and she was always approachable.

I was supposed to get some blood cultures done at 9.00 a.m., but the doctors had to put in a vas cath in a couple of patients for dialysis, so that takes priority. I do wonder what the rest of my life will be like off dialysis. I am still having a hard time getting used to that concept. I know life has got to be a hell of a lot better because of Lin's gift. I have really got to make the most of it. I feel so good at the moment, except that I need a good night's sleep. I am sure that will come in time.

I think I will be here next week because my creatinine and other levels aren't that stable, and the scar tissue needs to be healed better before I go back to Canberra. I don't want the surgeons in Canberra to touch me after all this.

On a lighter note, I said to the nurse from the dialysis ward that I would like to catch up with some of the old crew from years gone by. I might just be able to, which will be great. I'll be glad when the doctors start reducing the levels of CSA, prednisone, and Imuran. When they do that, I think I will feel more at ease going out or travelling around.

Thursday, 17 February 1994

My blood results from yesterday were a bit better. They seem to waver back and forth at the moment. I am sure it will take time to settle. I must admit that I am quite hungry these days, which is probably due to the prednisone, but my weight seems to be reasonable. I still haven't heard about when I get the rest of my clips out, so I will approach them tomorrow at the clinic. My white blood cell count was up again yesterday, but they don't seemed that concerned about it so I won't be.

I slept well last night and had a good day today. I have now got a TV in my room, so that should be a bit better. A friend rang today and said that I should come around. I thought I would wait till Saturday afternoon. She could come over to pick me up, and we could go back to her unit for afternoon tea. It will be good to get out of the nurses' home for a bit.

Spoke to some other friends last night, and they may come over on the weekend. They are great friends who helped me do gigs in Sydney at the Rocks before I went solo. I used to do a night with them once a week. We would rotate sets at the Mercantile Hotel. I also did similar nights with my brother Luke at the Observer Hotel in the Rocks.

Friday, 18 February 1994

Things are really picking up. The creatinine went down yesterday to 155, and my white cell count is getting better. It really looks as though everything is working well. Today they have reduced my prednisone to 20 mg per day, so that's another step in the right direction. I have to get some prescriptions for the medication, but that won't be a problem. Got a month's worth of tablets today, so that will keep things under control. With a bit of luck, the creatinine will be down again today, which will be another bonus.

It is strange that I haven't needed dialysis since the kidney started working on 4 February. It's been over two weeks – amazing.

Still have got sore feet though, like I am walking on glass. It only started since the transplant, so who knows what that's about? I must ask the clinic sister if this is part of the drugs or just me. [I later found out that one of the drugs I was on increased my uric acid, which meant I was in the early stages of gout.]

Got my insurance claim completed by the resident. Hopefully he is high enough to satisfy the insurance company and cover the bills. Just need some copies and then I'll send it off.

The clinic sister has got to take my clips out today and check my leg scar to make sure it will heal all right. Today I am feeling really well. I think it will still take time to get back to work, so I don't want to rush. The only reason I would go back is if I needed the money, but I should be taking it easy when I get back to Canberra.

Saturday, 19 February 1994

My creatinine went up again to 172 yesterday. I wish it would settle below 150, but it looks as though it will be jumping around for a while. I'm glad I am here in Sydney until things settle. I have to ring up at two to find out what today's results are, just to be sure before I go out this afternoon.

Sunday, 20 February 1994

After all of my concern yesterday, it appears that the creatinine went back down to 143, which is great. Over the last week my creatinine has not been stable, which means the CSA is still having an effect on the kidney. I'll be seeing the doctor tomorrow. It will be interesting to see what he has to say about it all.

I went to a friend's place last night for dinner. It was very pleasant, and it was great to get out of the nurses' home. She has always been a good cook, so the meal was fantastic. It was good just to talk about what is happening in someone else's life for a change, not just focus on how I am or the transplant. I got a chance to catch up on all the things that have been going on with our mutual friends while I have been in hospital. I headed back to the hospital about 9.00 p.m. as I am still getting used to being out and about.

Everything is looking great in my life at the moment. Lin has recovered really well from her operation, and it looks like Lin's kidney was destined for me.

Well, you won't believe it. I just found out that my potassium is – wait for it – 10. I can't believe it is that high because I don't have any symptoms. A normal potassium level is below 5.5, so who knows what happened? Anyway, I'm back at the hospital, just waiting to see what they plan on doing with me. I hope they have something else in mind apart from dialysis or Resonium, because I think I would probably need to drink a whole bottle of that stuff, and I don't intend to do that. My potassium can't be that high. There may be another reason.

[That Sunday afternoon, they took a blood sample and checked the potassium again. It was 5.6, so they gave me some Resonium to bring it down – not too much though, which was good. I don't know why the potassium was over 5, but it could have been the CSA.]

Monday, 21 February 1994

Today I saw the doctor, and he was very impressed with the levels. He was shocked at the abnormal potassium reading and put it down to lab error. The last result for the creatinine yesterday was 140. I should think that today it will be even less, which is great.

Last night I only woke up once to go to the toilet, so it looks like the bladder is settling down. I had been going three or four times a night. To think they were looking at connecting an external bladder because they were worried that my bladder wasn't going to work! I'm so glad that the bladder is settling down.

The doctors are very happy with the way things are going. The one I saw today said I could go home any time. I told him that I would head back to Canberra on Sunday, so I will have to make some arrangements.

I think I will be coming back to Sydney next year. I want to try my luck at the music scene again. We'll see what happens. I just have to try to get a transfer at work.

They have reduced the prednisone to three tabs per day. By the end of the week, that should be stable, and I can go back to Canberra with a relaxed feeling that I have done as much as I can to stabilise the kidney.

Tuesday, 22 February 1994

I am now going back to Canberra on Tuesday. A friend of mine is coming to visit his dad on Monday, and he will help me drive back in the afternoon on Tuesday. One thing that I want to find out about before I go home is to do with this pain in my scar. It is quite sharp, but I can't pick the exact spot. My headaches don't appear to have anything to do with my blood pressure, so I must get my eyes tested when I get back. I will mention these things to the clinic sister tomorrow and see what she says.

Slept pretty well last night, but this morning I am feeling a bit tired. Told the clinic sister about my aches and pains, and she says to tell doctors tomorrow.

[Later] I told the doctors about my aches and pains, and they have just as much of an idea as I do, so that doesn't really help. My weight was 73.6 kg, so I've lost a bit of fluid, which is good.

Friday, 4 March 1994

Guess what? I'm actually back in Canberra. My creatinine was 169 yesterday and keeps on jumping around. I really think things will work out fine. I got a letter from my uncle in England the other day, and he had some reassuring things to say. I can't make up my mind whether to go on a long holiday at the end of this year or go to Sydney or *what*. I seem to have soooo many options open to me at the moment. It's fantastic, but I may as well take each step at a time.

Sunday, 6 March 1994

This is the first weekend I've had off since the operation. It really feels that everything is going to work out fine. Over the last week I've been getting diarrhoea, but this morning I have been free of it so far.

I've got to drop into the Jazz School of Music tomorrow to find out if I can still do the second semester and organise some lessons with the vocal coach. The big band is basically no more as I don't have a bass player or keyboard player any more. I don't know what to do with the rest of the band, but I am sure it will be fine.

***

By the time this transplant came along, I was losing hope of ever getting off dialysis. Mentally, I found it very challenging. I had gotten to the point where I couldn't see my life going for much longer. My body was having a hard time, and I looked like death warmed up. I am so grateful to Lin for giving me her kidney!

I can't believe that was over twenty-two years ago. My creatinine eventually settled down after a while. The doctors realised that my body did not handle the toxicity of the cyclosporin, so they reduced it, and the creatinine levels stabilised in the range of 115 to 150.

My life has certainly moved on from those days on dialysis. In brief:

- I met the woman I was destined to marry towards the end of 1994.
- I travelled the world for six months.
- I got married to the woman I mentioned.
- I left my job in the public service.
- I was offered an IT contract in the UK, doing the job I had been doing in public service.
- I bought a flat near Notting Hill, London.;
- About five years after I got married, we got divorced.
- I travelled around the UK, working for various IT recruitment agencies and test consultancies. As part of those roles, I also visited areas of Europe and India.
- I ended up working as a managing test consultant for a large international consultancy firm, the ultimate goal I had set myself years before.

Unbelievable.

11

Life after the Gift

I certainly have tried to make the most of my new life. After the transplant in 1994, I had much more time, and it took me quite a while to get used to this fact. The transition was helped, to a degree, by the requirements to have regular blood tests at the hospital for the first twelve months. I also had a plan to travel again, but without worrying about dialysis.

I didn't have any excuses any more due to dialysis; I just had to get on and do it, which was a strange mindset to handle. It was like I was free but I didn't know how to be free. I had spent my life from 17 to 33 years of age being kept alive by a machine, with the support of my family, friends, and medical teams. Now I was on my own. It was weird for me, anyway.

My previous life had had so many constraints, including an 800 ml fluid restriction. Those constraints weren't there anymore. It took me some time to drink and eat what I wanted. As for my job in the public service, I wondered whether that was all I was going to do, even though I had achieved quite a lot in that role.

When I got the fifth transplant, my life seemed to open up to so many options that I didn't really know what to do. I was 33 years of age, and I felt 17! It was like my life had just begun again.

I knew I had made the most of my life with dialysis, but now I had an opportunity to do amazing things. Yet I had no clue.

I decided to take a leap and go travelling for six months to figure out what I wanted. I was still being monitored by the transplant team in Canberra. I had to make sure the kidney was stable before I started my travels.

The last time I travelled had been on dialysis in 1988, and this was seven years later, 1995. Communication was still by cards and letters. Most people still didn't have mobile phones or laptops. Those technologies were in their infancy, and available only to people who had money. I didn't have a computer except for the one at work, which ran on an operating system that was 1 megabyte in size. I didn't buy a PC for home use until after I got back from my travels, and then it had only a dialup connection to the outside world.

I planned to travel via the United States, as I wanted to see places I associated with the blues, jazz, and soul. During the time I was planning my holiday, a friend of mine broke up from her partner and was at a loose end, so I suggested that she join me on my tour. We ended up planning a fantastic trip. It was during the planning that I met my future wife, but the tour still went ahead. We went from Los Angeles to New Orleans to see the Blues &and Roots Festival for two weeks, then up to Chicago and New York. After the States, we went on to Europe.

It was a great trip around the States, and we met some great people along the way. We caught up initially with a couple of friends of mine in LA. We went to Universal Studios. My friends organised for us to go to the Magic Castle, where magicians put on shows for other magicians. Apparently one should be part of the magicians guild or get an invitation to attend these shows, so we were very privileged. Los Angeles was amazing and a great way to start our trip. We included a look at Venice Beach, where all the people who think they should be in movies hang out.

We flew to the Grand Canyon and went swimming in a pool at the bottom of a cliff. We could only get to the waterfall and pool by riding some American Indian reservation ponies to the top of a cliff and climbing down a metal chain through the cliff. That probably would not pass any safety inspection these days.

My Faithful Steed

I saw amazing ancient cities that had been carved into a cliff face by a forgotten American Indian tribe. The angles were perfect, according to our guide. We had an incredible experience on that tour.

New Orleans was also unbelievable. I was allowed to sing in a few bars along the way, from the Durango Blues Bar to B. B. King's Blues Club in Memphis. I also made a recording where Elvis Presley made most of his early his recordings – Sun Studios in Memphis.

Singing in B. B. King's Blues Club, Memphis

We spent about two weeks in New Orleans at the Blues and Roots Festival, and we had a fantastic time. The music was wonderful, and so were the food and the people we met. We took a side trip to Baton Rouge, which was different and quite run down, but that may have been the area that we ended up seeing.

We had one slight change in plan, which meant that I went to Chicago by myself. At the time I think it was the best option. My travel buddy fell for the bus driver, to the point that she wasn't really enjoying our stay in New Orleans. I said to her that she should probably meet up with the guy in LA, as that was where he was going, before it spoilt the rest of her holiday. After some discussion, she booked her ticket to LA and I headed to Chicago.

Chicago was fantastic, scary, and amazing. I was supposed to stay in the Intercontinental Hotel, as we had found a great deal in a travel magazine, but as my travel buddy wasn't with me, I wasn't sure if the deal would still be valid. To my surprise, the hotel had lost our reservation. I still had booking confirmation, so they honoured it and upgraded me to a king-sized suite, which I couldn't believe. I was in Chicago by myself, in a suite that I probably couldn't even afford today. Crazy. I felt guilty, after I checked in, that I had enjoyed luxury while I didn't know if my travel buddy had even arrived in LA. It turned out that she met up with the bus driver and it wasn't exactly what she expected. But she was glad I had encouraged her to find out. We met up again in New York and had a great time together.

There was a scary bit of being by myself in Chicago, and that was walking to Buddy Guy's club. It looked on the map as if it were just a few blocks from where I was staying. I found out that 'just a few blocks' in Chicago can take you from a pretty safe area to one where I probably should have taken a taxi. I also seemed to be the only guy in the audience who was from out of town. But the beer was good and the atmosphere amazing. It was a great band and night out, so I can't really complain.

The worst part was walking back by myself at one o'clock in the morning. It was dead quiet and there weren't many street lights. As I seemed to be the only one around at that time of night, I decided to head towards the lake. It was only a couple of blocks away, and it was better lit. Sometimes it's better to go with your gut feeling. I eventually made it back to the hotel, after seeing a different side of Chicago. The next few days were taken up by touristy stuff. I visited the Sears Tower and a few other blues clubs. It was fantastic.

By the end of the week in Chicago, I was ready to head to New York and catch up with my travel buddy again. While in New York, we met a retired judge and his wife. We got to meet them through an advert that my travel buddy found for meeting New Yorkers and getting a view from a local's perspective. We met the judge in a coffee shop, and he took us to his favourite Italian restaurant for lunch. Then he took us to an art gallery that his wife managed. After meeting his wife, we were invited back to their place for coffee. Then he escorted us back to the hotel. Could that happen today? I doubt it. I feel very privileged that we were introduced to a wonderful couple who were so welcoming.

After about a week in New York, we headed to London. My travel buddy decided to go back to Australia, as she had been asked to return to a job. I continued on my European tour after staying with my brother for a while, doing the tourist bit. I dropped my résumé at an agency to see if there was a possibility of getting work in the UK in test management – just another option for my future.

The European tour was amazing. Our tour group had a fifty-two-seater bus with only twenty-seven people on board. As I was traveling on my own I had to share a room with one of the other people on the bus. That was an interesting experience, but I lived to tell the story, so I guess it wasn't that bad. Still, I wished I were still travelling with my buddy from Australia; she was a lot more fun. The trip took thirty days, and we started in London.

The people on the tour were all pretty good, apart from a few married couples who seemed to want to complain about everything. Our first stop was Paris. We made our way through Spain via Madrid and Barcelona, which is one of my favourite cities in Europe. We enjoyed the French Riviera and Monaco, where we went to a casino in Monte Carlo. The girls on the bus took the opportunity to dress up, and they looked fantastic.

Holding up the Leaning Tower of Pisa

We travelled through Italy to Rome, Pisa, Pompeii, Sorrento, and Venice. I got to know the girls on the bus very well and had a great laugh on the trip, though nothing happened with any of them. I *did* have a girlfriend back home.

Rome was amazing with all the statues and architecture. The Colosseum brought back images of the movie *Ben Hur* with the chariot races. We saw some incredible scenery along the coast to Pompeii and Sorrento including the unusual and tragic sites in Pompeii from the aftermath of the volcanic eruption.

When we arrived in Venice, I couldn't believe all the buildings that were still standing in water after hundreds of years. The girls on the tour took the opportunity to get serenaded by gondoliers up and down the canals. Most of the guys just took photos of the architecture and a pigeon or two.

When we crossed into Romania, the tour guide and bus driver bribed the border guards to let us in. As we drove into the country, there were stalls on the side of the road that had dried red chillies hanging for sale. We didn't stop, as the driver didn't want to hang around the border too long.

The weather wasn't great in Romania – raining, windy, and very cold. When we had finished our tour, we stopped at a memorial of the last war. They had guards there, tossing rifles at each other across a twelve-foot gap. It was quite impressive, but I felt sorry for the guys having to do this for the tourists, no matter what the weather.

As we headed out of Romania, we were stopped at the border. Guards boarded the bus, armed with AK-47s, to check our passports. Unfortunately, due to the bribery episode coming in, we didn't have proper stamps. These guards were not very understanding. The discussion became quite heated, so the tour guide and bus driver took them aside, off the bus. I assume another bribe changed hands. In any event, they let us go through the border. I am sure things have changed since 1995, but it wasn't a very pleasant experience, especially for the girls. Still, we got through it without too much trouble.

We went to a schnapps museum in Austria. I decided I would sample all twenty flavours on the bar at the end of the museum tour. I was *drunk* by the end of that. I bought a bottle of 23 Carat Gold Schnapps and two shot glasses. The problem was that we had climbed a stepladder to get into the bar, and I was a bit concerned how I was going to get back down again. There was a ramp at the other end of the bar, designed for people who had a few too many schnapps. That was lucky for me. I made it down half the slope before the girls, who had also had a few drinks, had to help me the rest of the way. I dropped the shot glasses. Fortunately, I was able to catch them on my feet so they didn't break on the concrete. I was very lucky that day.

In Germany, we went to a beer hall. I decided I could drink about three litres of beer. Boy, was I sick that night. My roommate wasn't very impressed.

I took myself off the next day for some time by myself and caught a bus from East Berlin to West Berlin via the Wall museum. I met a lovely woman and her daughter on the bus. I started talking to them about what it was like to live in East Berlin in 1995 compared to how it used to be before the Wall was removed. She was of the opinion that there was some resentment building between the West and East Berliners. The West Berliners felt that the East Berliners were taking all the jobs, as they would work for less. I think there is still that concern to this day about migrants who come from the new EU countries to other countries in the EU. Anyway, the woman I met was lovely and opened my eyes a bit that day.

I was coming to the end of my European tour, and I'd had a great time. I kept in contact with one of the tour members. She and I got on really well, and she was in Melbourne. She was also a jeweller who offered to make some rings for me if I ended up proposing. I did propose to my girlfriend, and we got my friend from the tour to make the engagement and wedding rings.

After I returned from that amazing holiday, I settled back into my life in Canberra, which now included my girlfriend as well as work and, of course, my music.

The big band had pretty well dissolved while I was recovering from the transplant, but we had a few gigs when I got back. Now that I had a bit of time I started to work on another musical project, a solo CD. It took about twelve months to complete, as I decided to make the most of my time and figure out what I really wanted to do. I started a part-time course in networking to give me a bit of focus apart from my work, my bands, my girlfriend, and my CD.

I did try and keep the big band going, but I ended getting gigs for a reduced line-up known as the Phil Coleman Blues Band. I also continued with my solo work. The way things were looking, I would need the money. I was getting married, and within a year I had decided to take leave without pay from the public service to complete the networking course I had started.

I completed *The Gift* CD and launched it in May 1997 at the National Press Club in Canberra. The launch went really well, and I made a few sales on the night. I could not have completed the recording without the help of quite a few musicians that I had worked with over the years. My wife's encouragement was also crucial to completing the recording.

I didn't have the opportunity to promote the CD very much. Within two months of launch, I received a call from an IT recruitment agency in London. I had left my résumé with them and never really thought I would hear back. They contacted me about a senior test analyst contract role. By then I had been working on a test team for about eight years and was confident in my skills to perform the contract role.

Can you imagine how I felt? I was so excited, worried, and concerned, namely because I had just got married and started the networking course full-time. But what an opportunity.

I went ahead with the phone interview and was offered the job, starting in London on Monday, 16 July 1997 – two weeks from the time they confirmed that I had the role. The new job was in line with the role I had been performing, but the opportunity to work in London and earn double the salary of my current role was too good to refuse.

I had agreed with my wife that if I got the role, I would go over first and let her finish her diploma, as she was studying too. She could join me later if everything was going well. The next problem was that I had to convince my college that it was for the best for me to work in the UK, which they agreed. I had to sit three of my final exams early and actually took one over the phone when I was in London.

So there I was, working in London, studying for an exam, and wondering if my wife would ever come over to join me.

Then I got my diploma, my wife came over to London, and I had my first contract. Bloody amazing. I felt I was the luckiest man in the world. It was as if I were on a spaceship, leaving a life of suffering for a totally new universe where I could do nothing wrong. In less than three years I had gone from wondering if I was going to survive another day on dialysis to living in London and having brunch at the Waldorf on Sundays. I was living a life I had only dreamt of.

Things got better and better in London for the next few years. My wife got a job in a school library, which was exactly what she wanted. I got offered a better contract as a test manager at British Airways. We bought a flat near Portobello Road and were planning a trip to New York, flying the Concorde.

Then, over some time and several personal challenges, things started to go wrong. My wife and I decided to go our separate ways, which was the best thing to do at the time. Within a year of making that decision, we were separated and on our way to a divorce.

I was planning to return permanently to Australia after we got divorced. As part of that plan, I finalised a company that I had set up in the UK. When I came back to the UK after signing the divorce papers in Australia, I found out from my accountant that the tax office said I owed them a lot of money. It took me twenty-four months to convince them that I didn't owe them as much as they said. I never ended up going back to Australia. I think that too was the right decision at that time of my life.

A few years after I got divorced, my life started to improve. I moved up to the north of England to Sheffield, for a contract role in a major bank. I lived with a girl I'd met and her two children. I think we had a good relationship and a pretty good life for the six years we were together.

Eventually, I had to get a test consultancy role down south again, as the work up north was drying up. My girlfriend and I eventually went our separate ways after a while of trying a long-distance relationship. She met someone else and later had a little girl with her new partner, so things worked out for the best. I am still friends with her and her children, which is great.

Since that time I haven't been in a serious relationship. To be honest, my life tends to be easier when I'm on my own. Maybe I wasn't meant to be in a long-term relationship … but I never say never.

From the work perspective, things were going well. I ended up working for a consultancy back in London. Apart from work, I tried to settle down. I bought a house in Woking, Surrey, and decided to start learning salsa.

Life was really good. I was learning a lot, both in work and about myself. I had made some great friends, and most of those friends are still part of my life. The friendships I developed through salsa have now been an important part of my life for several years. I became quite good at dancing, even with my knee problem. I ended up auditioning for a movie and was selected as an extra in the comedy *Cuban Fury*, though in the end I only appeared on the cutting-room floor.

I worked around the country for my day job and went to India and Romania for client visits. I have always been very good at building a solid team and developing strategy for programmes I have worked on over the years. After several years, I had the opportunity to join one of the world's biggest consultancies. I was thrilled to be a managing test consultant for such a firm, and did what I could to build successful test teams and improve methodologies.

I worked around the country on several client projects. After several more years, the environment became more political. I found that all the travel and pressures from dealing with the political environment started to impact my health. I also found that my knee was not as strong as it used to be, which certainly didn't help. It was affecting my walking.

I really wanted to keep my job, but I could tell my health was suffering. I continued to travel for a couple of years before the doctors diagnosed the problem as being due to having hardly any cartilage left in my knee. That made it very painful to walk.

I also found that for some reason my legs were starting to go numb. The doctors weren't sure why that was happening. It was like everything was hitting me at the same time. It took time for all the tests and diagnostic work, and in the meantime I was on a lot of painkillers and other medication. I knew I wasn't handling work well because I hated getting up in the morning.

The combination of the knee pain, the numbness in my legs, and a stressful project at work made me realise that there was something else wrong, so I went to see my doctor. She signed me off work due to stress. This was really difficult for me to accept. I felt like a failure, even after all the other things that I had been through in my life. I had to accept that I had hit the wall. I ended up seeing a counsellor, who was great. She helped me through the problems.

On top of all the issues with work, I found out that my mother wasn't well. She needed a new place to live. I bought a house for her in Australia and thought that would help out, but I discovered later that she needed more support.

I still didn't really know what was going on with my legs. The doctors had not yet realised it had nothing to do with my knee. I knew the operation on my knee hadn't really helped.

I went back to work again after recovering from both the knee operation and the stress, but I knew my legs weren't right, They were still going numb. I also still had problems with my knee because my leg muscles weren't supporting it. My knee specialist believed that if I built up the muscles around my knee, I could avoid having a knee replacement. But no matter how much I worked my legs, the muscles around my knee didn't provide enough support.

About a year's worth of tests later, I learned that two discs in my spine had ruptured and were impacting the nerves in my spine. This was why my legs were going numb and my knee muscles weren't developing. When I went to see the neurosurgeon, he said that I was very lucky I could still walk.

They eventually decided to operate on the discs in my spine. I asked my sister to come over to look after me, which she did. I had never had an operation on my back before, and she had medical training. The operation went really well, and my legs stopped going numb, which was great. But they still weren't quite right.

After this disc operation, I went back to work again on a site where I had been several years before. I was travelling a lot again, but that was my job; I didn't really have an option.

About a year after I had my first disc operation, the numbness recurred. The doctors did another MRI and found there had been further deterioration in the discs. The surgeon suggested another operation to fix the problem.

Around the time of my second back operation, we found that my mother needed to go into a retirement home. I decided to take time off work before things got on top of me again. I went to see my doctor just to confirm the details of the operation, and to my surprise she signed me off on sick leave again. She said the more I travelled, the worse my back got, and I had to get my back and legs sorted.

I knew I couldn't keep on travelling, but unfortunately that was what I was employed to do. I went ahead and had my next back operation before I made any decision. After I recovered, I decided to resign from work. I needed time to recover fully, and I didn't want to feel guilty about work.

I am currently on a year's break from work – or, as I have called it, a sabbatical. I have written this book, seen Australia, and toured more of the United States. When I get back to the UK, I will decide what to do. Go back to work, maybe? Who knows?

I felt like a failure when I first went on dialysis, because I didn't like depending on people. I realise now that, given what I have gone through in my life, I am definitely not a failure.

I have tried to learn to accept help from people when I need to, but I still have trouble understanding my limitations. Accepting help is not an attribute of being a failure. Accepting help means having a realistic understanding of your limitations.

I've achieved most of the goals that I set myself early on, and still enjoyed life along the way. I may not have got the balance right all the way through, but maybe you don't have to be perfect all the time.

I think that I have met some wonderful people along the way, including some amazing women. Every one of them has had an impact on my life, and I have learnt a lot from them. I was not successful with my marriage, but one day the woman of my dreams will walk into my life. You just never know.

It's crazy to look back and see where I have come from. I can't believe how lucky I've been. I don't regret any decisions I have made, as I believe things have worked out for the best for everyone, including myself.

When I started on dialysis, I was 17 years old. I didn't think I would live past 25. Now I'm writing this book, sitting in a four-star hotel room in Paris, and drinking a bottle of water that would have equated to at least two days on my old fluid restriction.

I handed in my resignation on 28 January 2015 and formally left my job on 28 February 2015. I paid off my flat in Woking,

Surrey. I bought a retirement unit for my mum with the proceeds of the sale of my property in Goulburn, Australia, and my flat in Westbourne Park, London.

I don't know what lies ahead for me, but I don't believe my story is over yet.

Who would have thought I would reach 55 years of age? When I was 17, I sure didn't. Working on balance has been the key for me to enjoy my life to the full, and I'm still working on it. I hope you enjoy yours!

The End? Maybe!

Printed in the United States
By Bookmasters